ELECTRIC ROSARY

By Tim Foley

The first performance of *Electric Rosary*
was at the Royal Exchange Theatre, Manchester
on 23 April 2022.

ELECTRIC ROSARY

By Tim Foley

Mary	Breffni Holahan
Philippa	Suzette Llewellyn
Constance	Olwen May
Elizabeth	Jo Mousley
Child	Yandass Ndlovu
Theresa	Saroja-Lily Ratnavel
Director	Jaz Woodcock-Stewart
Designer	Charlotte Espiner
Lighting Designer	Simisola Majekodunmi
Composer and Sound Designer	Anna Clock
Assistant Director	Darren Sinnott
Voice Leader	Michael Betteridge
Fight Director	Kenan Ali
Casting Director	Julia Horan CDG
Company Stage Manager	Harriet Stewart
Deputy Stage Manager	Sarah Jenkins
Assistant Stage Manager	Emilia Stoddart
Stage Management Placement	Frances Ashton
Dramaturg	Suzanne Bell
Bruntwood Coordinator	Chloe Smith

Breffni Holahan (Mary)

Breffni Holahan has won multiple awards such as The Stage Award for Acting Excellence 2019, and Best Performer Dublin Fringe 2019. Some recent theatre credits include: *Collapsible* (Ellie Keel Productions for The Bush Theatre, The Abbey Theatre, and HighTide), and various productions for leading Irish theatre companies including: The Abbey Theatre, MALAPROP, Collapsible Horse, Rough Magic, and Anu Productions. Recent screen credits include *The Nevers* (HBO), *Joan Verra*, *The Racer* (both Blinder Films), *Vikings* (MGM/History Channel), and *Everything Not Saved* (RTE).

Suzette Llewellyn (Philippa)

Suzette Llewellyn trained at LAMDA. Theatre credits include: *Running With Lions* (Talawa); *Cat on a Hot Tin Roof* (ETT); *Chigger Foot Boys* (Tara Arts); *Hellscreen* (Vaults Festival); *The Multiple Myrtle Mysteries* (Dulwich Festival); *Urban Afro Saxons* (Talawa); *Whale* (Royal National Theatre); *Midsummer Night's Dream*, *Comedy of Errors*, *Golden Girls*, *Children of a Lesser God* (Wolsey Theatre). Television includes: *EastEnders*, *Holby City*, *Doctors*, *Hold The Sunset*, *The Dumping Ground*, *Fearless*, *The Coroner*, *Casualty* (BBC); *Top Boy* (Well Street Productions); *The Windsors* (NOHO Film & Television); *Catastrophe* (Avalon Television); *Rocket's Island* (Lime Pictures). Film credits include: *Real* (Small Long Productions/ Fizz & Ginger Films); *Faces* (Dreamcoat Productions); *Molly Moon* (Amber Entertainment); *Manderlay* (Zentropa); *Baby Mother* (Formation Films/C4); *Playing Away* (Insight/C4).

Olwen May (Constance)

Olwen May has worked across theatre, television, radio, and film. Theatre credits include: *Saint George* (Royal National Theatre); *Operation Black Antler* (Blast Theory); *Band of Gold* (Rollem Productions); *The Crucible*, *Richard III*, *Romeo and Juliet* (Leeds Playhouse); *Tender Bolus – Hunger for Change*, and *Orpheus Descending* (Royal Exchange Theatre); *The Importance of Being Earnest*, *The Good Person of Szechuan*, *Independent Means*, *Private Fears in Public Places*, *A Doll's House* (Manchester Library Theatre). Television credits include: *Leaving* (Apple TV); *A Very British Scandal*, *Care*, *Bodyguard*, *Happy Valley* (Series 1&2), *Inspector George Gently*, *Casualty 1909*, *The Forgotten Fallen*, *Silent Witness*, *Florence Nightingale*, *Life on Mars 2* (BBC). Film credits include: *God on the Rocks* (Skreba Films); *My Son the Fanatic* (Zephyr Films); *Seeing Red* (Granada Films). Radio credits include: *Craven*, *Bright Day*, *The Mayor of Casterbridge*, *Top Girls*, *A Winter's Tale* (Radio 4); *The Threepenny Opera* (Radio 3).

Jo Mousley (Elizabeth)

Jo Mousley is a founder member of Hear the Picture, an actor-led creative and immersive audio description company. Theatre access credits include: Sheffield Crucible, SBC Theatre of Sanctuary and The Watermill, Newbury. Theatre credits include: *Hello and Goodbye* (York Theatre Royal); *Four Minutes Twelve Seconds*, *The Father*, *David Copperfield* (Oldham Coliseum); *Road*, *Europe*, *Hamlet*, *Be My Baby*, *A Christmas Carol* (Leeds Playhouse, Pop Up Ensemble season); *Tom's Midnight Garden* (Theatre-by-the-lake-Keswick); *Relatively Speaking*, *Saturday Night, Sunday Morning* (Oldham Coliseum/Harrogate); *Two*, *Brassed Off* (Derby Theatre); *The Twits* (Leicester Curve/Rose Theatre/ UK Tour); *Barnbow Canaries* (West Yorkshire Playhouse); *Corrie!* (UK and New Zealand Tour); *The Full Monty* (UK Tour); *Horrible Histories/ Horrible Christmas* (Birmingham Stage Company); *Blood and Chocolate* (Slung Low/York/Pilot); *Arabian Nights* (Library Theatre Company); *Ugly*, *Forgotten Things*, *Riot Rebellion and Bloody Insurrection* (Red Ladder); *Blood Wedding* (Liverpool Playhouse/Cut to the Chase). Television credits include: *Hollyoaks* (Lime Pictures); *Emmerdale* (ITV Yorkshire); *Monroe* (ITV); *Coronation Street* (ITV); *Nice Guy Eddie* (BBC). Radio: *The Common Pursuit* (BBC Radio 4).

Yandass Ndlovu (Child)

Yandass Ndlovu studied at Arden School of Theatre and is the founder of I M Pact collective. Acting credits include: *Macbeth*, *Jubilee*, *Our Town*, *Birth Orchid* (Royal Exchange Theatre); *Dead Certain* (Hope Mill Theatre). Dancing credits include: *Alphabus*, *WOZA*, *Icaria-NOWNESS*, *FlexN Manchester*, *Sea Change* (Manchester International Festival); *Nike Air-Shimmer* (Size? & JD Sports); *Boy Blue Elavate* and *See Me After-PUSH* (HOME); *FlexN Young Identity* (Contact Theatre); *Danny Beard* (Manchester Pride 21); *Yandass.mov, Run Boy Run* (Channel 4, Random Acts short films). Choreographer credits include: *The Walk/ When Birds Land – Little Amal* (Manchester International Festival); *Everything All of the Time* (Contact Theatre). Credits in movement direction include: *Bloody Elle* (Royal Exchange); *Vuka* (Manchester Museum). I M Pact Productions and collaborations include: *All I Want for Christmas* (Royal Exchange); *LET'S GO* (Film); *Vuka* (Manchester Museum); *Resilience* (Lowry).

Saroja-Lily Ratnavel (Theresa)

Saroja-Lily Ratnavel is an actor and writer from the Isle of Man. She trained at LAMDA and graduated from the MFA acting course in 2021.

Prior to this, she studied English Literature at Durham University where she graduated with a First Class BA (Hons) degree. Theatre credits include: *Name, Place, Animal, Thing* and *The Key Worker's Cycle* (Almeida). Credits whilst training include: *The Christians, Europe, The Tempest* and *Women Beware Women*. She recently made her television debut in *Bravo Two Charlies* (BBC) and was featured in the final series of *D For Dexter* (BBC Radio 4).

Tim Foley (Writer)

Tim Foley is a playwright based in Manchester. His work includes: *Electric Rosary* (winner of the 2017 Bruntwood Prize Judges' Award; premiered at the Royal Exchange Theatre, Manchester, in 2022); *Astronauts of Hartlepool* (2017 VAULT Festival, winner of the VAULT Origins Award for Outstanding New Work); and *The Dogs of War* (Old Red Lion Theatre, 2015). In 2016 he won the OffWestEnd award for Most Promising New Playwright. Tim also writes audio drama set in the worlds of *Doctor Who* for Big Finish Productions. His original podcast, *North West Footwear Database*, was featured on BBC Radio 4 Extra.

Jaz Woodcock-Stewart (Director)

Jaz Woodcock-Stewart is a theatre director and artist and is the Artistic Director of award-winning arts company, Antler. She won the Jury Prize for her production *Civilisation* at Fast Forward Festival and has been the finalist for several directing awards: Genesis Future Directors Award 2017 and 2019, the RTST Sir Peter Hall Director Award 2018 and the JMK Award 2016. Her theatre credits include: *Gulliver's Travels* (Unicorn); *Fen* (LAMDA); *Learning Piece* (The Place); *Civilisation* (Hellerau, New Diorama, HOME Manchester); *Lands* (Bush Theatre); *Wifmon* – writing attachment (National Theatre Studio); If I Were Me (Soho Theatre, Antler). Other credits include: as Assistant Director: *All About Eve* (Noel Coward Theatre, Sonia Friedman Productions); as Staff Director: *Network* (National Theatre) and as Resident Director: *Lazarus* (King's Cross Theatre).

Charlotte Espiner (Designer)

Charlotte Espiner has worked extensively as a designer in theatre and film across various disciplines, including new writing, devised work, dance, opera and musicals. Her designs have appeared at many venues across the UK and abroad. Theatre Design credits include: *Civilisation* (New Diorama/HOME/Staatsschauspiel Dresden);

Error Error Error (Marlowe Theatre/RSC); *Heart of Hammersmith* (Lyric Hammersmith); *Let Loose* (ENB/The Unicorn); *Grimm Tales* (Online, The Unicorn); *The Merchant of Venice* (Sainsbury Theatre, LAMDA); *The Winter's Tale* (Sainsbury Theatre, LAMDA); *The Changeling* (GBS Theatre, RADA); *Civilisation* (Underbelly, Edinburgh); *The Highs and Lows of Owning Your Own Home* (ACUD, Berlin); *Pufferfish* (The Cage, VAULT Festival); *Lands* (Bush Studio); *Parents' Evening* (Jermyn Street Theatre); *A Play About My Dad* (Jermyn Street Theatre); *Acis and Galatea* (St John Smith's Square); *Kingdom Come* (RSC); *Summerfolk* (Vanbrugh Theatre, RADA); *Home Chat* (Finborough Theatre); *Adler&Gibb* (Summerhall, Edinburgh/The Unicorn/The Lowry/Kirk Douglas Theatre, LA); *It is Easy to be Dead* – Olivier Award nomination (Finborough Theatre/Trafalgar Studios). Film credits include: *Stand Still* (Island Pictures); *The Rain Collector* (Wigwam Films); *Lizard Girl* – BAFTA award winner (BBC); *Double Take* (BAFTA/Channel 4); *Paper Mountains* (Ruby Productions); *Mirror* (Ruby Productions).

Simisola Majekodunmi (Lighting Designer)

Simisola Majekodunmi graduated from RADA with a specialist degree in Lighting Design. Her work in theatre includes: *Traplord* (180 Studios); *Jungle Rumble* (Fortune Theatre); *Human Nurture* (Sheffield Theatres); *The Wiz* (Hope Mill Theatre); *Is God Is* and *Living Newspaper Edition 6* (Royal Court Theatre); *J'ouvert* (Theatre503, Harold Pinter Theatre); *Lucid*, *Tiger under the skin* (New Public Company); *Driving Miss Daisy* (York Theatre Royal); *Invisible Harmony* (Southbank Centre); *Just Another Day and Night* (The Place Theatre); *Seeds* (Leeds Playhouse). Her work as an associate includes: *The Shark is Broken* (Ambassador's Theatre); *Carousel* (Regent's Park Open Air Theatre); *Shoe Lady* (Royal Court Theatre); *15 Heroines* (Jermyn Street Theatre); *Herding Cats* (Soho Theatre).

Anna Clock (Composer and Sound Designer)

Anna Clock trained at Trinity College Dublin, Royal Irish Academy of Music and Central School of Speech and Drama. Theatre credits include: *The Beauty Queen of Leenane* (Lyric Hammersmith), *Crave* (Chichester Festival Theatre); *Mum* (Theatre Royal Plymouth/Soho Theatre); *Another Planet* (Lakeside Arts, site specific digital); *Mystery Trip* (Nigel & Louise, digital); *The Effect* (English Theatre, Frankfurt); *I Wanna Be Yours* (Paines Plough/Tamasha, UK tour, Bush Theatre); *Not F**kin' Sorry*, *Shuck 'n' Jive*, *Soft Animals* (Soho Theatre); *Admin* (Vault Festival, Live Collision, Dublin Fringe Festival); *Armadillo* (The Yard); *Fatty Fat Fat* (Roundhouse/Edinburgh Festival, UK tour); *Mary*

and Maria (Camden People's Theatre); *Twelfth Night* (Southwark
Playhouse). Anna has composed for the RTE Contempo quartet,
Tonnta, New Dublin Voices, Kirkos, Node Ensemble, Dulciana,
Gamelan Nua and Téada Orchestra.

Darren Sinnott (Assistant Director)

Darren Sinnott is currently training at Birkbeck University. His
previous directing credits include: *Butterflies Of Life* (Jermyn St
Theatre & Pleasance); *Speak Softly, Go Far* (Abbey Theatre & Dublin
Fringe); *Admin* (Dublin Fringe Festival, Winner – First Fortnight Award,
Outburst Arts, Belfast; Vault Festival London). Other credits include:
Associate Director for *Once Before You Go* (Gate Theatre, Dublin);
Assistant Director for *Nora: A Doll's House* (Royal Exchange Theatre);
Farm (WillFredd Theatre, touring); Creative Associate for *ATOMU* (VR,
Sundance Film Festival at Jermyn Street Theatre 2020-2021).

Michael Betteridge (Voice Leader)

Michael Betteridge is a composer and choral conductor based in
Manchester, UK. Specializing in working with young and leisure
time music makers, as well as working in theatrical settings, he
has led choral and opera performances across the UK and abroad
most often giving new works their premieres, including some of his
own. After studying composition at the Royal Northern College of
Music he was one of the first recipients of Sing for Pleasure's Young
Conductors Programme in 2013. Since then, he has premiered works
across a range of genres by Finn Anderson, Anna Appleby, Dominie
Hooper and Philip Venables, amongst many others. In April 2016 he
conducted the world premiere of Andrew Keeling's community opera
Get Weaving at the Bridgewater Hall in collaboration with Chetham's
School of Music for over 200 performers. He is artistic director of The
Sunday Boys – an open access low voiced LGBTQ+ choir based in the
heart of Manchester.

Kenan Ali (Fight Director)

Recent theatre credits include: *The Mountain Top*, *Death of a Salesman*,
The Producers, *Mother Courage and Her Children*, *Wuthering Heights*,
Rockets and Blue Lights, *Nora: A Doll's House* (Royal Exchange Theatre);
Oliver Twist (Leeds Playhouse); *Guys & Dolls*, *Standing at the Sky's
Edge*, *A Midsummer Night's Dream* (Crucible Theatre, Sheffield); *Kes*,
Treasure Island (Octagon Theatre, Bolton); *Beauty and the Beast* (New
Vic Theatre, Stoke) ; *Romeo & Juliet*, *Peter Pan* (Hull Truck Theatre);

Treasure Island (Stephen Joseph Theatre, Scarborough); *Mother of Him* (Park Theatre); *Lost Boys* (National Youth Theatre). Feature film credits include: *Blank* (Kenmor Films), *Soldiers of the Damned* (Viking TV & Film). Short film credits include: *Incompatiable* (directed by Maxine Peake), *Sisters* (Home), *The Wilds* (Sea & Sky Pictures); *Girl Alone*, *Circuit*, *Moment of Grace* (Old Hall Films); *Rabbit Punch* (Rabbit Punch Film). Television credits include: *Stad* (S4C Wales).

Julia Horan CDG (Casting Director)

Julia Horan has worked in casting across theatre, film and television. Theatre credits include: *Wife of Willesden*, *Pass Over*, *Red Velvet* (Kiln Theatre/Tricycle, West End/St Ann's Warehouse). *Macbeth*, *The Duchess of Malfi*, *The Doctor*, *Three Sisters*, *The Wild Duck*, *Machinal*, *The Writer*, *The Treatment*, *Oil*, *Uncle Vanya* (Almeida); *The Jungle* (Young Vic/West End/Curran San Francisco); *Blood Wedding*, *Jesus Hopped the A Train*, *Fun Home*, *Yellowman*, *Wings*, *Life of Galileo*, *Once in a Lifetime*, *Blue/Orange*, *The Trial*, *Ah, Wilderness*, *Man*, *Happy Days*, *Public Enemy*, *The Shawl* (Young Vic); *Appropriate* (Donmar Warehouse); *Summer And Smoke*, *The Twilight Zone*, *Hamlet*, *Mary Stuart*, *Oresteia*, *Chimerica* (Almeida/West End); *All About Eve*, *Harry Potter And The Cursed Child* (West End); *The Inheritance* (Young Vic/West End); *Yerma* (Young Vic/Park Ave Armory); *The Slaves of Solitude* (Hampstead); *Cat on a Hot Tin Roof* (Young Vic/West End); *Obsession*, *Hamlet* (Barbican); *City of Glass* (59 Prods); *Tipping the Velvet* (Lyric Hammersmith); *Martyr* (Actors Touring Company); *The Seagull* (Regent's Open Air); *The Boy in the Striped Pyjamas* (Chichester Festival Theatre); *The Nether* (Royal Court/West End); *A View from the Bridge* (Young Vic/West End/Broadway); *Spring Awakening*, *The Seagull* (Headlong). Recent Film/TV includes: *Together*; *Hamlet*; *Why it's Kicking off Everywhere*; *The Exception*; *Departure*; *The Trial – A Murder in the Family*.

Manchester's Royal Exchange Theatre Company transforms the way people see theatre, each other and the world around them. Our historic building was taken over by artists in 1976. Today it is an award-winning cultural charity that produces new theatre in-the-round, in communities, on the road and online.

Exchange remains at the heart of everything we make and do. Now our currency is brand new drama and reinvigorated classics, the boldest artists and a company of highly skilled makers – all brought together in a shared imaginative endeavour to trade ideas and experiences with the people of Greater Manchester (and beyond).

The Exchange's unique auditorium is powerfully democratic, a space where audiences and performers meet as equals, entering and exiting through the same doors. It is the inspiration for all we do; inviting everyone to understand the past, engage in today's big questions, collectively imagine a better future and lose themselves in the moment of a great night out.

The Royal Exchange was named Regional Theatre of the Year in 2016 and School of the Year at The Stage Awards 2018. Our work, developed with an incredible array of artists and theatre makers, includes *Hamlet* with Maxine Peake (for stage and film), *The Skriker* (with the Manchester International Festival), *King Lear* (co- produced with Talawa Theatre Company, filmed for BBC iPlayer and BBC Four), *The House of Bernarda Alba* (a co-production with Graeae), *Our Town* (directed by Sarah Frankcom), *Light Falls* (a world-premiere from Simon Stephens directed by Sarah Frankcom with original music by Jarvis Cocker), *Wuthering Heights* (directed by Joint Artistic Director Bryony Shanahan), *Rockets and Blue Lights* (by award-winning writer Winsome Pinnock and directed by Miranda Cromwell), *The Mountaintop* (Digital Streaming directed by Joint Artistic Director Roy Alexander Weise), *All I Want For Christmas* (digital commission for December 2020), *Oh Woman!* (digital commissions for International

Women's Day 2021) and *Bloody Elle – A Gig Musical* (directed by
Bryony Shanahan).

Find out more at
royalexchange.co.uk
facebook.com/rxtheatre
instagram.com/rxtheatre
twitter.com/rxtheatre
youtube.com/rxtheatre

For the Royal Exchange Theatre

Connecting Team
Andy Barry
Rosie Bingham
Duncan Butcher
Oceana Julie Cage Nzene
Philippa Crossman
Millie Dhillon
Neil Eskins
Inga Hirst
Fallon Mayne
Alfie Mulroy
Paula Rabbitt
Sharon Raymond
Scarlett Spiro-Beazley
Liam Steers
Leo Timoney
Roy Alexander Weise
Bianca Danielle
Carys Williams

Facilitating Team
Matt Averall
Yvonne Cox
Rachel Davies
Steve Freeman
Alex Healey
Michelle Hickman
James Howard

Sharon Lever
Sheralee Lockhart
Mike Seal
James Webster
Freya Wilkinson
Vicky Wormald

Making Team
Halima Arteh
Suzanne Bell
Hannah Blamire
Amy Chandler
Richard Delight
Tracy Dunk
Louis Fryman
Travis Hiner
Felicia Jagne
Matt Lever
Bryony Shanahan
Jo Shepstone
Matthew Sims
Chloe Smith
Sorcha Steele
Jack Lancelot Stewart
Martha Tomlinson
Katie Vine
Mark Distin Webster

the bruntwood
prize for playwriting 2017
in partnership with the **Royal Exchange Theatre**

Winner

A partnership between the Royal Exchange Theatre and property
company Bruntwood, the Prize is an opportunity for writers of any
background and experience to enter unperformed plays to be judged
by a panel of industry experts for a chance to win part of a prize fund
totalling £40,000.

At the heart of the Bruntwood Prize for Playwriting is the principal
that anyone and everyone can enter the Prize – it is entirely
anonymous and scripts are judged purely on the basis of the work
alone and with no knowledge of the identity of the playwright.
Since its inception in 2005 over 15,000 scripts have been entered,
£304,000 has been awarded to 34 prize winning writers and 26
winning productions have been staged in 38 UK wide venues. In
2015 it celebrated its 10th anniversary and is now recognised as a
launch-pad for some of the country's most respected and produced
playwrights.

Each winner enters into a development process with the Royal
Exchange Theatre in an endeavour to bring their work to production.
It is not guaranteed but we aspire to produce each play and find
co-producers to give the plays a longer life and further reach. There
have been co-productions with Lyric Hammersmith, Live Theatre,
Soho Theatre, Bush Theatre, Orange Tree Theatre, Sherman Theatre,
High Tide and the Royal Court Theatre. Work has also gone on to be
produced internationally from Australia, USA, Germany, France, to
Canada and Sweden.

The Bruntwood Prize for Playwriting is a genuine endeavour to
discover new stories and help playwrights develop their craft,
providing everybody and anybody with the opportunity to write
a play. It offers a fantastic opportunity to hone your writing skills,

whether or not you have written for the stage before (35% of the entrants to the 2017 Prize had never written a play before). In addition to a high proportion of winning and shortlisted plays being produced professionally, each of the top 100 plays receives individual feedback from the Royal Exchange Theatre's creative team.

Donors and Supporters

Principal Partners

Corporate Partner
Bruntwood

Corporate Sponsor
Edwardian Hotels
Electricity North West
Galloways Printers
Garratts Solicitors
Irwin Mitchell
Warner Media

Principle Corporate Member
Edmundson Electrical
Regatta

Encore Corporate Member
Ralli Solicitors LLP
Torevell & Partners

Associate Corporate Member
5plus Architects
Brewin Dolphin
HFL Building Solutions
Sanderson Weatherall

RXIGNITE Collective
Ben Caldwell & Becky Rosenthal
Ellen Hanlon
Garratts Solicitors
Irwin Mitchell
Martyn & Valerie Torevell

Our Trailblazers
Jason Austin
Arnold & Brenda Bradshaw
Meg & Peter Cooper
Barbara Crossley
John & Penny Early
Mike Edge & Pippa England
Ellen Hanlon
Richard & Elaine Johnson
Jack & Janice Livingstone
Carolyn & Andrew Mellor
Stuart Montgomery
Anthony Morrow & Family

Carole Nash OBE
Stephen & Judy Poster
Anthony & Margaret Preston
Tim & Jennifer Raffle
Nicola Shindler
& all our anonymous patrons

Our Firelights
John Batley
Mr J Bishop & Mr J Taylor
Angela Brookes
Ron & Gillian Brown
Paul & Ann Cannings
Grace R Dutt, James Poole & Lena
  Poole
Mark Evans
Mrs V Fletcher
Nigel Gourlay
Irene Gray
Roy & Maria Greenwood
Geoff & Jennie Holman
Malcolm Pitcher & Helen Gilman
Robin & Mark Taylor
Helen & Phil Wiles

Special Acknowledgement to
Arnold & Brenda Bradshaw
Barbara Crossley
Susan & Sally Hodgkiss CBE

Trusts and Foundations
The Backstage Trust
The Beaverbrooks Charitable Trust
The Esmée Fairbairn Foundation
The Garfield Weston Foundation
The Granada Foundation
The Noël Coward Foundation
The Holroyd Foundation
The Jigsaw Foundation
The John Thaw Foundations
The Oglesby Charitable Trust
The Peter Henriques Foundation
The Paul Hamlyn Foundation
The Rayne Foundation
The Victoria Wood Foundation

ELECTRIC ROSARY

Tim Foley

Acknowledgements

Tim Foley

Writing a play is a team effort. So there are a lot of people to thank.

Thank you to those in religious orders who have assisted me with this story. Thanks especially to the brothers of Nunraw Abbey who gave me the initial inspiration, and the sisters of Tyburn Convent in Hyde Park, a key influence for the Sisters of Grace.

I couldn't have written a first draft without the backing of the Channel 4 playwright-in-residency scheme and the unconditional support of Pentabus Theatre Company. They gave me the writer's holy trinity: time and space and money. Thank you especially to Sue Higginson, who ran the scheme; Elizabeth Freestone, who gave this fledgling story the encouragement it needed; and Jenny Pearce, for the washing machine.

Thank you to the Bruntwood Prize. That changed everything.

I've had some amazing actors read the script for me. Melanie McHugh, Maggie O'Brien, Nathalie Barclay, Judith Roddy, Sally Armstrong, Michelle Butterley, Sharon Duncan-Brewster, Nadia Emam, Kelly Hotten, Kate Layden, Norah Lopez Holden, Celia Keenan Bolger, Layla Khosh, Susannah Perkins, Kathleen McNenny, Kecia Lewis, Ellen Parker, Charlie Hardwick, Rosa Hesmondhalgh, Lois Chimimba, Maxine Finch, Alexandra Mathie, Islam Bouakkaz, Samantha Power, Danielle Henry, Sandra Cole, Georgia Frost, Zoe Armer, Akiel Dowe. These readings were arranged by, among others, Sophie Motley, Teddy Bergman, Suzanne Bell, Elizabeth Freestone. Thank you all.

Thank you to the various readers of various drafts. Shout outs to Brendan Macdonald, my secret weapon, may he read everything I ever write; Stewart Pringle and all at the NT Studio for their support (thanks also to Simon Longman, my neighbour, for the falafel); Joe White for helping a tipsy me decide on the title at Latitude. If you want to hear the alternatives, buy us some more drinks.

Thanks to the potential cast and crew of the cancelled 2020 version. Circumstances robbed us but I hope I've done you proud. I've mentioned Elizabeth Freestone a couple of times already – she is very much embedded in the world of the convent. I imagine she lives in a farm a few fields over.

Thank you Bryony Shanahan and Roy Alexander Weise for giving this play a second life (fitting for an Easter story). A huge huge thank-you to Suzanne Bell, who has been this play's biggest supporter since day one. It would not be happening without her persistence.

Thank you to Jaz for your brilliance and your curiosity. I couldn't have done this with anyone else. Thank you to all the cast and crew of the 2022 version. I won't be able to properly articulate how much your talent and dedication means to me for a very long time, but know that the words burble inside me and threaten to overwhelm me with tears.

Thank you to my grandad, for setting me on this path.

Thank you to all my friends, who provided shelter in the glade.

And thank you above all else to Martin, my rock.

4

Characters

ELIZABETH, *Acting Mother*
CONSTANCE, *Sister*
PHILIPPA, *Sister*
THERESA, *novice*
MARY, *robot*
CHILD, *martyr*

Place & Time

St Grace's Convent, rural Britain, near future.
The story begins on Shrove Tuesday and ends on Easter Sunday.

Setting

Most of the action takes place in a large chapel room. It's no
longer a place of worship. There are boxes of junk and religious
remnants, including the Lesser Relics. Large windows look out
over the convent's farmlands. Two exits, one leading inside, one
outside. The room is damp and draughty. You'll struggle to find
God.

*This text went to press before the end of rehearsals and so may
differ slightly from the play as performed.*

Notes on the Play

(*Beat*.) is short, (*Pause*.) is long, punctuation is pacing.

When binary is spoken, 0 is pronounced *oh*, not *zero*.

Some of Mary's dialogue is in quotation marks. This is sourced from other places and the actor's performance may reflect this.

ACT ONE

17 February – *Shrove Tuesday*

Late afternoon. It's raining.

Plastic chairs in a circle. A small trolley sits nearby holding a teapot, a pile of cakes, and a photo of the Old Mother. There is a projector hooked up to an old laptop. Buckets squat around the room.

PHILIPPA *sits in the circle, head down, holding her bottle of pills. She takes one.*

THERESA *stares out of the window with binoculars.*

THERESA. Oh! (*Pause.*) Oh! (*Pause.*) Oh!

PHILIPPA. What is it Theresa

THERESA. All the letters are just – oh!

PHILIPPA. We'll stick them back on when the weather's better

THERESA. We've lost the C, the O – both Ns of CONVENT! Now it just reads, 'ST GRACE – VET'. I know she's holy and everything but I don't know how good she is with animals. What if the letters are lost for good? Swallowed in the mud? Nothing good about that. 'Lost for bad', that's what we should – oh! 'ST GRACE E.T.' – she's an alien now!

PHILIPPA. Enough of all that, start stacking the chairs

PHILIPPA *starts stacking the chairs.* THERESA *keeps staring out.*

THERESA. But that's why nobody's here, isn't it?

PHILIPPA. Yes, our patron saint came and beamed them all away

THERESA. They've no sign to guide them –

PHILIPPA. We've ten minutes till vespers –

THERESA. They're lost in the fields, they're stuck in the rain –

PHILIPPA. Theresa. Nobody's here because nobody cares

THERESA. People care Sister Philippa! There were plenty at
    the funeral

PHILIPPA. Plenty? Twenty

THERESA. There were more than twenty

PHILIPPA. I counted, precisely twenty

THERESA. Twenty's good. Twenty-one, if you, count the Old
    Mother

PHILIPPA (*beat*). When you tot up attendance at a funeral,
    Theresa, don't include the departed. It's assumed they'll
    be there. You can make silly remarks like that to me, but if
    Sister Constance hears you –

THERESA. No no no I know. (*Beat.*) Where is, Sister
    Constance?

PHILIPPA. No idea. I've texted her

THERESA. Is that why Mother Elizabeth stormed off?

PHILIPPA. Possibly. Probably. That and the lack of, of, doesn't
    help. We'll be alright. My aches and pains are going away.
    And you be on your best behaviour this evening

THERESA. Will everyone be miserable?

PHILIPPA. We won't be by compline. (*Gestures to trolley.*)
    Need to eat all these before tomorrow. Brace yourself for a
    sugar rush, we'll be bouncing off the walls for days

    Thud thud thud on the ceiling.

    I see Sister Patricia has started, I took her up a sweet bun
    earlier

THERESA. Oh no. So did I

PHILIPPA. Two buns deep, we've well and truly lost her

THERESA. Are we still having pancakes?

PHILIPPA. On top of all of this?

THERESA. Penance and Pancakes, it's tradition

PHILIPPA. Oh, if it's tradition

THERESA. And that's why nobody came. They're clearing out their cupboards and laughing in their kitchens. It's the last happy day for a while

CONSTANCE *enters from the rain. Dripping wet, speckled with mud. She's haunted by terrible news, but she'll tell no one.*

CONSTANCE. I know Christ can walk on water, but even He would struggle in this mud. (*To* THERESA.) Lord Almighty girl, sort that hair out. When was the last time you polished your shoes?

THERESA. Sorry Sister Constance

CONSTANCE. I presume you're giving up standards for Lent

THERESA. I'm giving up sugar

CONSTANCE. Shouldn't give up anything at all. Make yourself useful for once, learn a new skill. Any skill, for that matter. I need to learn how to evade technological oppression. Use those goggles to watch the Reapers girl, they're creeping ever closer

PHILIPPA. They're doing no such thing

CONSTANCE. I assume this was you, Philippa. (*Holds up mobile.*) Deftly slipped upon my person, so you can keep a track of me

PHILIPPA. So you can stay in touch, Sister Constance

CONSTANCE. And how am I meant to do that when your words dissolve into a random string of letters? Looks like that blasted sign out there

THERESA. Oh!

PHILIPPA. Is she still an alien, Theresa?

THERESA. Yes but she's not a saint any more

CONSTANCE (*peers at phone*). 'Where r u', well I get that bit,
'E v x'?

PHILIPPA. 'Elizabeth very cross'.

CONSTANCE. Oh is she now, why, she see the state of this
one?

PHILIPPA. If we're discussing anybody's appearance – but
we're not getting into that, we're going to work together and
get this cleared up

CONSTANCE. Not as though we have prayers here any more

PHILIPPA. That doesn't mean it should go to wrack and ruin.
The projector?

CONSTANCE. What about it?

PHILIPPA. Will you pack it away?

CONSTANCE. I've no idea how it works

PHILIPPA. Does that prevent you from putting it in a box?

CONSTANCE. I've just got back, give us a moment

   PHILIPPA *goes to the projector.*

THERESA. Sister Philippa – before you – could we watch the
slideshow again?

PHILIPPA. We don't have time Theresa –

THERESA. Just the pictures of the Old Mother in Ecuador. We
can imagine we're with our sisters out there

PHILIPPA. We will be soon enough

CONSTANCE. Don't start with all that

PHILIPPA. Summer will be here before we know it

CONSTANCE. I'm not convinced there'll be summer again

THERESA. Oh but there will be Sister Constance, and we need to be prepared! The sunny weather. The glorious walk. We'll take the pilgrim's path and rest in the beautiful gardens, the beautiful beautiful gardens! Yes, the best rest. And it'll be so bright! We'll bathe in the light of the Lord! I'm re-reading all their postcards. Looking at the pictures. One of them is a photo of a statue of the little baby Jesus in a Panama hat!

CONSTANCE. Aye, looking forward to all that scrimping and saving. Can't wait to buy you a ticket

THERESA. Thank you Sister Constance

CONSTANCE. A one-way ticket

THERESA. Oh thank you thank you! So let's look at the photographs one last time Sister Philippa. We might even cheer up Mother Elizabeth!

CONSTANCE. Acting, Mother

PHILIPPA (*beat*). I'll give you the laptop later Theresa, peruse them at your leisure, but right now we don't, look, just, leave this to us, go check on Sister Patricia, make sure she hasn't got crumbs all over her bed

THERESA. Yes Sister Philippa

THERESA *exits*.

PHILIPPA *puts away the projector.*

CONSTANCE. 'Crumbs'. Did you give Sister Patricia a bun

PHILIPPA. We gave her two buns

CONSTANCE. Lord Almighty. Restraint, Philippa, restraint. And don't go giving Theresa the laptop

PHILIPPA. We're not the ones avoiding 'technological oppression'

CONSTANCE. Things like that, they're a distraction

PHILIPPA. They're a motivation. Where've you been all day?

CONSTANCE. Had a prior engagement. Did anybody turn up to this charade?

PHILIPPA. Nope

CONSTANCE. Aye well I could've told you that

PHILIPPA. Think you did, repeatedly. What kind of prior engagement?

CONSTANCE. A private one. And I confessed to Father O'Gorman. Mainly listened to his own grievances. He's having trouble burning the palms in all this. Getting flashbacks to last year's charity barbecue. He knew nothing of this little gathering, by the way

PHILIPPA. You were asked to invite him

CONSTANCE. I'd never do that. We had the funeral, we had the wake, what's this one, third time lucky?

PHILIPPA. Elizabeth wanted to do something public-facing

CONSTANCE. 'Public-facing'. Is that why the buckets – are they for donations?

PHILIPPA. We're leaking in here now –

CONSTANCE. That's why there were so few at the funeral, Elizabeth charging for entry –

PHILIPPA. She was doing no such thing

CONSTANCE. Then maybe she should've done. If she's gonna do what she promised, we need a full-on charity appeal

PHILIPPA. She has a plan. (*Beat.*) The buckets could do with emptying

CONSTANCE. Aye, so could I. But I'm not going to the bathroom in this, it'll be flooded again and I'm not sorting it

PHILIPPA. I can't do everything around here

CONSTANCE. I'm back now, I can help

PHILIPPA. Then let's clean up before vespers

CONSTANCE. Aye. Just let me get my breath back

PHILIPPA. How did this place survive without me?

CONSTANCE. It didn't. (*Beat.*) It did

PHILIPPA *continues tidying, placing the photo on a side table.*

THERESA *enters.*

THERESA. Sister Patricia's fine, she's sleeping

PHILIPPA. Crashed already then, small mercies. Oh, that reminds me. (*Pulls out phone.*) Need to email the doctor

CONSTANCE. Why?

PHILIPPA. See if they can deliver her prescription

THERESA. Why can't we collect it any more?

PHILIPPA. The Old Mother was the only one who could drive. Unless you've hidden your light under a bushel and you're a dab hand at a manual

THERESA. Can it really not drive itself?

PHILIPPA. It really can't

CONSTANCE. I wish it could, we'd put you in the boot and tell it to keep going

PHILIPPA. Sent. Five minutes to vespers people –

THERESA. Wait I bumped into Mother – Acting, Mother, Elizabeth. She gave me a message

CONSTANCE. Doesn't deign to deliver it herself

THERESA. She's delaying the start of vespers by ten minutes

CONSTANCE. She's what?

PHILIPPA (*looks at phone*). Oh yes, just come through on the calendar

CONSTANCE. Delaying the start of vespers? What right does she have to – to interrupt the day like that, to interrupt our sacred duty. Is this her new regime? Playing fast and loose with the schedule? What else is she gonna do?

THERESA. She's going to get a robot

CONSTANCE. She. (*Beat*.) I need you to repeat that girl

THERESA *throws her hand over her mouth.*

PHILIPPA. Theresa

THERESA. I wasn't to mention the last bit! I wasn't to know!
When I say I bumped into her, I sort of walked in on her in
her office and she was on the council website and she was
booking it up and she said not to say cos she's announcing it
at supper

CONSTANCE. She's announcing it at supper? She's
announcing it at supper!

PHILIPPA. She might have just been browsing

CONSTANCE. And why would she be browsing, for a robot!

PHILIPPA. Clearly we'll discuss it at supper

CONSTANCE. It's not up for discussion! A robot. In the
convent! What did I say girl? What did I say? Technological
oppression! (*Gesturing with phone*.) Having this on me all
day, gave me shivers all over

PHILIPPA. It vibrates when you get a text

CONSTANCE. And this, this is nothing compared to, to – one
of those lot out there, coming in here

THERESA. It's gonna be a lot more advanced than a Reaper,
that's what the Acting Mother –

PHILIPPA. Theresa

CONSTANCE. They're advancing all the time girl! One day
they'll march in here and cart us out of our beds

PHILIPPA. As long as they make them afterwards, I'm not
complaining

CONSTANCE (*beat*). Did you know about this?

PHILIPPA. The council are running an integration scheme –

CONSTANCE. You knew about this

PHILIPPA. And it comes with a sizeable bursary. What were you just saying about a charity appeal? That money will help pay for Ecuador

CONSTANCE. What are we gonna do when it comes in here, dressed as a nun?

PHILIPPA. It won't partake in any of the, vocational duties, obviously, just assist with the housework

CONSTANCE. The housework, is part of, the vocational duties. I'm not against a, a new recruit, as it were, these past, what, eighteen months with Theresa have been a, well, aye, it's been a long eighteen months

THERESA. And I have loved every minute of it

PHILIPPA. You can speak to Elizabeth about recruitment, but if we're being pragmatic –

CONSTANCE. We should vote on it. Without a unanimous decision –

PHILIPPA. And it wouldn't be unanimous –

CONSTANCE. So we shouldn't have a vote on it? There goes democracy! No wonder there are so many rumblings outside if this is the example we set. The Old Mother will be turning in her grave

PHILIPPA (*beat*). Theresa, Sister Patricia is banging on the floor again

THERESA. I don't think she is –

PHILIPPA. Theresa

THERESA. Yes Sister Philippa

THERESA *exits*.

PHILIPPA. Is this an argument to have in front of the novice?

CONSTANCE. I'll have it in front of everyone! These robots. Recording. Tracking. Never mind all that, they're just plain wrong

PHILIPPA. Next you'll be saying some of them have six toes

CONSTANCE. Aye, well, maybe they do. I listen to the streams

PHILIPPA. If you hear that on the news, you hear the wrong
    kind of news

CONSTANCE. S'no wrong kind of news

PHILIPPA. Luddite propaganda

CONSTANCE. Don't call it that

PHILIPPA. Call it what it is

CONSTANCE. Call it common sense if anything

PHILIPPA. Well they have the same number of toes as we do

CONSTANCE (*beat*). How about their x-ray eyes?

PHILIPPA. You believe all this nonsense?

CONSTANCE. Do I believe the reports, the research –

PHILIPPA. If you went in the farmlands, saw the Reapers up-
    close –

CONSTANCE. Out there, do what you like. But in here? No.
    S'unnatural

    CONSTANCE *roots around in a nearby box. She makes a
    mess.*

PHILIPPA. What are you doing now?

CONSTANCE. Who is she to be summoning robots? She's not
    even Mother yet! Something else we've not voted on

PHILIPPA. She didn't push it back on purpose –

CONSTANCE. So you're blaming poor Patricia? Whilst stuffing
    her full of buns

PHILIPPA. I'm not blaming anyone

CONSTANCE. We should be blaming Elizabeth. She's only
    Acting Mother, she shouldn't be –

PHILIPPA. Acting as Mother?

CONSTANCE. Aye. Well aye alright but still. Where are the blasted things?

PHILIPPA. If you told me what you're looking for –

CONSTANCE *pulls out a handful of prayer cards.*

CONSTANCE. Ah! We used to give these to the girls. We'll read this litany tonight

PHILIPPA. I think Elizabeth's already chosen one –

CONSTANCE. Litany of St Anthony. We pray for lost things, like decency, common sense. I wonder what the Church will make of this. Father O'Gorman will come along, douse the thing with holy water, hopefully rust the circuits

PHILIPPA. Look outside. Water doesn't stop them

CONSTANCE. Aye. There should be real workers out there. This rain. The end of days. When I was coming back just now, I felt the wet earth shift beneath me. It wasn't the mud, it was. No I don't know. I'm being daft. She's being dafter. I have such a bad feeling about this

PHILIPPA. Then we pray

CONSTANCE. Aye. Pray. I'm starting vespers. At the correct time

PHILIPPA. We're children of God, sister. No hunk of metal could replace any one of us

Songs of vespers.

The chairs are cleared away.

PHILIPPA *brings flowers to the Old Mother's 'shrine'.*

9 March – *Feast Day of St Frances of Rome*

Mid-morning. Still raining, but not as heavily as before.

In the centre, MARY *is slumped. There are traces of her packaging.*

ELIZABETH *stands beside her and studies a tablet.*

ELIZABETH. On. On. (*Beat.*) Go on. (*Reading, muttering, inaudible.*) 'When activated – See Activation. Activation, activation...' Need to make the font bigger, how do I... (*Pinches screen.*) That's too big. Small. Small. (*Beat.*) That's too small

ELIZABETH *puts the tablet down and walks across the room. She notices the flowers. She admires them – then catches herself admiring them.*

(*To* MARY.) I tell her not to waste these lovely flowers in here. I should ask her to remove them. Interrupting our Lenten requirements. (*Beat.*) You are too, I suppose. You shouldn't have arrived before Easter. They said last week we had no choice with the slots, but I made perfectly clear... No matter. It's all God's will. And just in case it isn't... I'll get the sisters at lunch to say an extra Hail Mary

MARY. Hello

ELIZABETH (*beat*). You're awake

MARY. I am awake

ELIZABETH. How long have you – I was reading the, information, to switch you on

MARY. Do you require 'information, to switch me on'?

ELIZABETH. Well, not now. How did I. Why did you speak?

MARY. I speak to communicate

ELIZABETH. No, I – why did you speak just now

MARY. I responded to my name

ELIZABETH. You responded to your – hang on hang on, there was something about that in the – (*Retrieves tablet.*) User Manual, yes, 'Assignation' (*Scrolls.*) assignation, assignation –

MARY. Do you require assistance?

ELIZABETH. I can do this on my own. (*Inaudible.*) 'To commence the primary phase this unit must be primed to yadda yadda yah…' (*Louder.*) 'And your robot's name is' ah ha, 'revealed in Section A, click here to', I didn't click it. (*Clicks.*) 'Mary'

MARY. Hello

ELIZABETH. You're called Mary

MARY. Hello

ELIZABETH. Will you say that every time I say, Mary?

MARY. I stop when you are sufficiently greeted

ELIZABETH. Right! You're very… It's not as though I was expecting, whizzing and beeping, but. The Reapers can't talk. And you talk… rather well

MARY. Thank you

ELIZABETH. You're welcome

MARY. My speech will develop, the more I listen. I will learn by example, adapt to your requirements

ELIZABETH. How, considerate. Well

ELIZABETH *picks up and rings a small bell.*

Here we go then. Um, welcome, Mary

MARY. Hello

ELIZABETH. How do we. I'm not sure I. Do you have any questions?

MARY. Why did you ring the bell?

ELIZABETH. No I meant, bigger questions, like uh, 'Where am I?', 'What am I doing here?'

MARY. You are in St Grace's Convent, you are talking to me

ELIZABETH. No I, uh. Well, if you really want to, the bell, when we used this room for services, it signified the Holy Spirit was present. Now it just lets someone know I want tea. Oh but I don't want tea. I did that, automatically. I ask for a pot whenever we get visitors and for a moment you. The leaps and bounds we make in a lifetime, eh? I had a Tamagotchi as a child, blew my mind. I haven't kept up with, all these new things, I'm afraid. There must be a word for it. Like a vegan, but for digital things. You could almost be mistaken, for one of us. Not quite. Nobody here can wake up as swiftly as you

MARY. I woke up in 1.1 seconds

ELIZABETH. Oh gosh

MARY. I apologise for the slow speed

ELIZABETH (*beat*). Is that a, joke?

MARY. Yes

ELIZABETH. I couldn't even stand up in 1.1 seconds, I should be so lucky

MARY. Would you like me to time you?

ELIZABETH. Is that another joke

MARY. You can reduce my humour output

ELIZABETH. Can I improve it?

MARY (*beat*). 'I should be so lucky'

ELIZABETH (*beat*). We need to think about your attire. The full habit would be inappropriate, but there's a man with a blog who'll take some pictures in a day or two, and you need to look like part of the. I suppose we'll dress you as a postulant. I keep asking the others to sort through all this, but there'll be a spare tabard in one of the. Of course it's a little ridiculous, but they want a big fanfare in the press about the scheme, part of the, terms and conditions. Not exactly sure what that'll achieve, there was another demonstration just a week or so ago against the, uh, people like your good self, but. It'll be good to remind the locals, we're here. And you're here too. Though I'm not sure everyone is pleased about it

MARY. Would you like me to find out?

ELIZABETH. Find out?

MARY. If 'everyone is pleased about it'

ELIZABETH. And how would you go about that

MARY. I monitor behavioural responses, verbal, non-verbal, I assess their emotional state

ELIZABETH. Very talented I'm sure. But I'm thinking of one sister in particular… and assessing her emotional state is tantamount to poking a large bear with a sharp stick. (*Gestures to packaging.*) I'll, clear this up

MARY. I will assist you

ELIZABETH. No no, I'll manage

MARY. Why?

ELIZABETH. Sorry?

MARY. Why 'manage'

ELIZABETH. Because I need to manage, I am, the manager, if you like

MARY (*beat*). You are reluctant to assert your authority

ELIZABETH. Excuse me? Where did that come from?

MARY. The flowers. 'These lovely flowers', 'I should ask her to remove them', 'should', rather than 'will', suggests uncertainty, suggests leniency, suggests insecurity. (*Beat.*) I will assist you –

ELIZABETH. I don't need your assistance! What a, an incredible assertion. Based on what, a slip of the tongue?

MARY. I monitor your behavioural responses, verbal, non-verbal –

ELIZABETH. Then stop it. This is outrageous, I should switch you off right now. 'Should', yes, I heard it. (*Sighs*.) You're no Tamagotchi, that's for sure

MARY. Would you like me to lower my perception field?

ELIZABETH. No, I. (*Beat*.) Raise it. I can't see the beam in mine eye, but clearly you can. If you get all that from, watching, listening. I wonder what you make of the rest of us. I haven't, introduced myself, I'm S–, I almost said Sister then, Mother, Elizabeth

MARY. You are the manager, you are the Mother

ELIZABETH. But I'm not the Mother, not yet, things are a little. (*Sighs*.) It's rather complicated

MARY. I can cope with 'complicated'

ELIZABETH (*beat*). Well the usual hierarchy is, suspended at the moment, due to the passing of the previous… It was very sudden, she didn't name a successor – not that that would be, binding of course, but a predecessor often gives a, a spiritual indication, a suggestion of authority – and we didn't even get that. Managed a last request though. Something everybody heard. But the Holy See made me Deputy a few years back since I am, or was, the treasurer here, I suppose that position will have to be reassigned, so it's fallen on me to assume the, uh, the, the. (*Beat*.) Look at you, listening to me witter on here

MARY. I am listening

ELIZABETH. No I mean, well no, thank you, for listening. (*Beat*.) We'll be back to normal after Lent. Once we've had the vote. The appointment of a Mother Superior is a, unfortunately, a strict, somewhat archaic, procedure, and the rules, I don't have them to hand, but they, uh –

MARY. 'No one may vote in place of another'

'No one outside the convent may be present'

'No one may reveal her vote once her ballot is cast'

ELIZABETH. How do you know all this?

MARY. I have access to your cloud. Information, 'the vote'

ELIZABETH. Oh. Yes of course the, so you can just? Mm-hmm. The rules preclude Sister Patricia from partaking, she's bed-bound at the moment and, there are good days, there are bad days, we agreed to wait until. She was better. But she, uh, she's not getting better, and looking ahead...

MARY. She will die

ELIZABETH. I wouldn't put it quite so bluntly. She'll, make her ascension when the Lord deems fit

MARY. When will 'Sister Patricia' die

ELIZABETH. You can't ask me that

MARY. I will access her medical records

ELIZABETH. No no don't do that, don't, pry

MARY. All information remains confidential. I can provide medical assistance

ELIZABETH. Can you?

MARY. My skill-set contains, basic diagnosis, reviewing prescriptions, preparation for surgery – palliative care

ELIZABETH. But that's. That could surely, relieve a burden. Not that Sister Patricia is a, please don't tell anyone I –

THERESA *enters with the tea tray. She stops in her tracks when she sees* MARY.

THERESA *silently mouths 'Is this the robot?'*

What was that Theresa?

THERESA. Nothing. Hello. (*Silently mouths again, 'Is this the robot?'*)

ELIZABETH. I've no idea what you're trying to say

MARY. She asks 'Is this the robot?'

THERESA. Oh!

ELIZABETH. Don't gawp, Theresa. I don't want tea. I suppose I'll have a cup. Theresa, if you could pour me a? And tidy away the... no, wait. Mary. Would you, um? Assist me?

MARY *clears packaging.* ELIZABETH *and* THERESA *observe her.*

She can meet the other sisters at lunch. Actually, what's the? Oh! We must prepare for midday prayers. Never mind about the tea Theresa, shame to waste it, but you ought to clear it away. Mary, if you, wait here, are you happy to wait?

MARY. I am 'happy to wait'

ELIZABETH. We'll carry on afterwards

THERESA. Mother Elizabeth, I was –

ELIZABETH. Yes?

THERESA. If you, my request for Lent. To learn a new skill

ELIZABETH. Not now Theresa

THERESA. I'm sorry

ELIZABETH. No no, I don't mean to be, short. We can't afford a driving instructor, that's the simple truth –

THERESA. Today is the feast day of St Frances of Rome and she is the patron saint of automobile drivers and I've got a big book of saints and there's a picture of her driving a car –

ELIZABETH. Walking is good for us. And I like these, online food deliveries. So there's no real need to drive into town, except Mass. And if it's raining, we take the bus

THERESA. They stopped the bus

ELIZABETH. They what? Why did they stop the bus?

THERESA. I don't know. They just stopped it. The news said the Luddites said –

ELIZABETH. No no. If we don't know, we don't listen to hearsay. 'He said she said', that isn't news, is it? Tidy this away and I'll see you in the chapel. Goodbye Mary

MARY. Goodbye Mother Elizabeth

ELIZABETH *exits*.

THERESA *starts to clear the tea but is distracted by* MARY.

THERESA (*pause*). I've just poured tea, and I'd feel really rude if I didn't offer you tea, so if someone was to do that, offer you tea, that someone being me, can you physically drink it?

MARY. I can physically drink it

THERESA. Wow. Okay. Tea. How do you usually take it

MARY. I do not 'usually take it'. This is my first cup of tea

THERESA (*beat*). I feel responsible now, I'd have made it a good pot if I'd known. Not that it won't be a good pot. May not be the best pot. We'll start you off with lots of milk and half a sugar

THERESA *makes the cup of tea. She pours the milk, spoons the sugar.*

MARY. Do you take 'lots of milk, and half a sugar'?

THERESA. I do! Maybe a few more sugars, guess how many sugars

MARY. One

THERESA. No. (*Giggles.*) Guess again

MARY (*glitches*). One

THERESA. No

MARY (*glitches*). One

THERESA. No, but one and one and one make three, that's how many sugars for me! (*Beat.*) Are you okay?

MARY. I am, refreshing

THERESA. You'll feel a lot more refreshed after this

THERESA *hands over the cup of tea.* MARY *holds it.*

You just sort of – in your mouth

MARY *drinks it in one gulp*.

You must be able to do such wonderful things. I heard about a robot who could walk through walls and they tried to make that sound like a bad thing, but I thought, that's great, we don't need doors any more

MARY. I am a basic model

THERESA. Don't be putting yourself down

MARY. It is a fact. I have, limitations

THERESA. Mustn't focus on the things you can't do, but the things you can. The Old Mother taught me that. I know one of your talents already – you can stand extreme temperatures. You downed a really hot cup of tea!

MARY. It was not 'really hot'

THERESA (*beat. Feels pot*). Oh I really messed up your first tea. Sometimes the kettle clicks and it doesn't do anything. This is terrible tea

MARY. Perhaps 'one of my talents' is to drink 'terrible tea'

THERESA (*giggles*). You're funny. So you'll stay here while we all – I wish I had time to give you a tour. I'll speak very quickly – this room, used to be the big chapel but now we all fit in the little chapel upstairs and it's much much warmer, so this is, well it's nothing really. In the boxes we have the Lesser Relics, which used to be upstairs, but now we're up there they're down here cos I know they're sacred remnants of our holy martyrs but nobody wants to look at their bloody hankies and toenails. Oh goodness I hope it's not a sin to say that, we all think it. We need to hang them up. The Reapers are in the fields all day. I think Sister Philippa worked them too hard before she brought them to the convent cos they all look a bit fed up. What do you think of the view?

MARY. The window is dirty

THERESA. In our convent in Ecuador, they have the most beautiful stained-glass windows and every day someone cleans each piece with a toothbrush

MARY. Should I clean the window 'with a toothbrush'?

THERESA. Not this one, no, we'll need something bigger than that. But don't look at, the glass, look through it. It's all God's earth and it's very very pretty but I think He made this bit a little bit sad. So we won't have to miss it when we go away this summer

MARY. Who is in the garden?

THERESA. Where? The Reapers can't come this close. It's not your reflection, is it? I've done that before. I used to sneak from the school and stare inside. Look at me now. Staring out

MARY (*beat*). My vision is, refreshing

We hear the songs of midday prayer. THERESA *bolts and skips towards the door.*

THERESA. They've started without me! I'll get such a scolding. Um, help yourself to terrible tea. I'll teach you how to make a better pot I promise

MARY. I know how to prepare tea

THERESA. Do you really?

MARY. It is in my skill-set

THERESA. That's amazing. What else can you do?

MARY. Would you like me to list my abilities?

THERESA. Later, yes, I want you to tell me everything. Wait – hang on – can you, drive a car? A manual

MARY. It is in my skill-set

THERESA. You have given me such an idea. Maybe I can learn by example as well

Midday prayer song swells through the space.

MARY *starts to hang the relics.*

*

A pause in the song as PHILIPPA *arrives with a mop.*

As she cleans, she narrates her actions:

PHILIPPA. Firm grip. Figure-eights. Quick soak. Thorough wring. Repeat

MARY. Your instructions may be formed in full sentences

PHILIPPA. I'll keep it nice and simple, thank you. Don't need you to be clever. Just need you to clean. Let's see you in action then

PHILIPPA *hands* MARY *the mop and directs her.*

PHILIPPA. Firm grip. Figure-eights. Good. This is. Oh, yes, you'll need to compensate for the floor, it's on a slight angle

MARY. The surface is imperfect

PHILIPPA. Ha. Aren't we all

MARY. No

PHILIPPA. I see we're going to have lots of fun with you! Quick soak. Thorough wring. Yes, you'll do nicely. My husband had to spend months fine-tuning the Reapers, you're clearly a later model. Even if you are second-hand, few scuffs on the. Never mind, all cosmetic. Carry on here and I'll check on your progress after vacuuming. We're going to get twice as much done now. Place is going to be sparkling

PHILIPPA *exits. The song continues.*

MARY *carries on mopping. She spies the flowers. Bins them.*

10 March – *Feast Day of St Anastasia the Patrician*

Early afternoon. The rain is slowing.

MARY *is now in her postulant tabard.*

She's reliving her smiles for the photograph – but ceases when ELIZABETH *enters.*

ELIZABETH. I thought that went well, very well! It's going to be a lovely photograph. Even if Sister Constance is scowling in the background. Did you hear what the man called us?

'Very progressive'. If this goes some way to reassuring the general public… I was considering, what you were saying yesterday. 'Palliative care'. With the photos done, I was just going to put you in the school, sorry, the shed, docking shed, with the Reapers. I only took you on for the bursary. Not that it stretches far. But if we kept you indoors for Sister Patricia… we can cut the costs of a private nurse… we can say that was my idea

MARY. You wish to 'cut the costs'

ELIZABETH. We're saving up. For Ecuador

MARY. You wish to purchase Ecuador

ELIZABETH. Ha! We'll settle for part-time residents. We fly out. This summer. To Ecuador, El Rosario, our sister convent

MARY. There is nothing in your calendar

ELIZABETH. Yes well, I'll, get round to putting it in at some point –

MARY. When do you fly?

ELIZABETH. I am yet to choose a date. Soon

MARY. 'Soon'. 'This summer'. Your projected income is insufficient to travel 'this summer' –

ELIZABETH. Not so loud please! I need to, work on it. I need to work on it. (*Beat.*) Insufficient

MARY. Yes

ELIZABETH. To the point of non-existent

MARY. Yes

ELIZABETH. You don't pull any punches do you

MARY. My skill-set does not contain the ability to hurt, damage, mutilate, kill –

ELIZABETH. No no I meant. Gets a little feisty at tea-time but. One thing at a time. If you can make this place more cost-efficient… There's uh, emails, donations, accounting files, can you keep a track of those?

MARY. I will assist you

ELIZABETH. Can you, assist even further? We take turns with the cooking, the cleaning, if we were, more economical there. We have a small income from our farmlands, that's Sister Philippa's domain but I oversee distribution, deliveries, that sort of thing. Would any of that – I mean, can you help with, some of this as well?

MARY. I can help with all of this

ELIZABETH. All?

MARY. I learn by example, adapt to your requirements. I will assist you

ELIZABETH. If that's, true… you'd really be a Godsend

25 March – *Feast of the Annunciation*

Supper time. It's stopped raining outside.

CONSTANCE *sits alone. She closes her eyes and clasps her hands. Prayer will not come.*

MARY *enters. After a moment,* CONSTANCE *notices.*

MARY. I'm interrupting you

CONSTANCE. You're interrupting nothing

MARY. I was sent to retrieve you. I'll leave you to pray

CONSTANCE. I'm not praying. I'm sure what we do all looks the same to you, I could be deep in reverent thought, but nope, it's indigestion. No idea how Theresa can mess up a plate of spaghetti hoops. The Lord did not bless that girl with much ability

MARY. You don't eat with the others

CONSTANCE. You don't eat at all

MARY. I could if required

CONSTANCE. Aye, well, don't. Down to our emergency tins, delivery vans blockaded again. I can starve to death in the meantime, cos Lord knows I'm not having hoops. Is there something you wanted, or did you just come to spy on me?

MARY. I'm not spying on you

CONSTANCE. You've been skulking around the place ever since you got here. Or worse, you're with Theresa, skidding around the courtyard

MARY. Her driving is improving

CONSTANCE. Improving? Two days ago she drove into the bins. I'm surprised our Glorious Leader is letting this happen. Bewitching her with your increasing eloquence. You'll be careful on our roads, can't talk your way out of trouble there. They are, after all, blockading the likes of you

MARY (*beat*). I was sent to retrieve you. The others wish to speak to the sisters in Ecuador

CONSTANCE. They wish it, aye. The connection's rarely strong enough

MARY. It is strong enough. I improved it. The stream will go through me

CONSTANCE. Good for you. Still not interested

MARY. They wish to commemorate the Old Mother –

CONSTANCE. It's an excuse to plan their visit. Getting excited. Can't be dealing with that

MARY. You do not want to go

CONSTANCE. Course I do. Chance to be closer to God, better weather to boot. But it's months off yet. If it happens at all. I know what Elizabeth's doing. Ecuador's a mission, not a manifesto. S'no way to run a convent

MARY. You do not think she should run the convent?

CONSTANCE. Huh. Yes, she's not truly Mother yet, is she? Someone else might throw their hat in. I've been here longer. I'm certainly wiser. And I wouldn't string my sisters along

MARY. You would make an inadequate Mother

CONSTANCE. Oh would I?

MARY. I have assessed your leadership potential. You isolate yourself

CONSTANCE. Why, cos I eat my meals alone?

MARY. You withhold information

CONSTANCE. What do you mean?

MARY. You receive private emails and you do not share their contents

CONSTANCE. So you are spying on me

MARY. I am monitoring you

CONSTANCE. And I know who's really doing the monitoring. How dare she pry. She can't read them, can she?

MARY. No. (*Beat.*) I'm sorry

CONSTANCE. You're 'sorry'? And who've you nicked that from? Can't imagine it was Elizabeth, never stoops to an apology. She could be sorry, if she chose to be. And she might be forgiven. You can't. You wouldn't mean it. You don't mean anything. (*Beat.*) Is there anything else

MARY. Yes

CONSTANCE. That's a polite way of saying 'go away' –

MARY. There is something else

CONSTANCE. What is it

MARY. Where is your God

CONSTANCE (*beat*). Just a simple question then

MARY. Where is your God

CONSTANCE. Why are you asking?

MARY. You say you will be 'closer to God' in Ecuador. I don't understand

CONSTANCE. Then it's not for you to understand. Ecuador's a holy place

MARY. El Rosario

CONSTANCE. Yes

MARY. The sister convent

CONSTANCE. Yes

MARY. Why

CONSTANCE. Because it is

MARY. Why

CONSTANCE. Cos some of our sisters. The Old Mother made a pilgrimage and she. I'm not telling you

MARY. Why

CONSTANCE. I'm in a lot of pain and I've no time for nonsense

MARY. Why are you in pain?

CONSTANCE (*beat*). Look. Long time ago the Old Mother left to do some missionary work. She went to South America and on her journey she stayed in a village called, El Rosario. The days were long and the work was hard and she found herself, getting sick. But she'd wander out at night when it was cooler. To feel the breeze from the grove. And on one of these, wanderings, the Old Mother found herself on a trail through the forest. Tired from her trek, she fell asleep by a large rock. And whilst she slept, the Mother had a vision. The forest is full of light. Not from the sun, but something much brighter. She sees a child, standing barefoot. And this majestic youth, they lead our Mother to a glade. And in the clearing, there's the Virgin Mary, all our long-gone sisters, they're smiling, laughing, singing songs about the Lord.

The Mother awoke, thinking it a dream. But that morning she
found the clearing again. There were footprints in the ground.
And the sickness in her body, in her soul, had gone. Gone. So
when you take the trail, you touch the foot of the rock, you
pray for someone's soul, and they're cured of all ill

MARY (*pause*). 'Someone's soul'

CONSTANCE. Aye. (*Beat*.) Could've found all this online,
there's a page on our website

MARY. Yes. Do you believe it?

CONSTANCE. Do I what?

MARY. The vision

CONSTANCE. Of course

MARY. How did the Old Mother know it was real

CONSTANCE. What?

MARY. What if she was misperceiving? What if she was
wrong?

CONSTANCE. The Old Mother was never wrong. See, you'll
never understand. No comprehension of what a miracle
is. It's something, outside science, and you are bound by
science, your mind's a, whaddaya call it, a closed circuit.
Now if we've stopped messing around in here –

CONSTANCE *stands. Ah, but she's in pain. She winces,
steadies herself, sits back down.*

MARY. I will assist you

CONSTANCE. No

CONSTANCE *fully rises. She hides her pain better.*

I'll join the others. All this talk of Ecuador, I. May as well,
pop in

MARY. I will accompany you

CONSTANCE. No. Wait here. Ponder on the nature of miracles.
And let's pray that blows a fuse or something

CONSTANCE *exits.*

MARY. 'Let's pray'. (*Beat.*) 'Let's, pray'

MARY *looks around and clasps her hands together –
echoing* CONSTANCE.

*

The lights flicker, the relics shudder.

MARY *sees the lights from the forest, feels the breeze from
the grove.*

*The world around her shivers. We see a projection of the
video call from Ecuador. Nuns smiling, laughing, singing
songs about the Lord…*

MARY *stares at them, she unclasps her hands to reach out
and –*

*

Evening. ELIZABETH *stands by* MARY.

ELIZABETH. Mary? Mary?

MARY. Yes Acting Mother

ELIZABETH. You were miles away

MARY. Ecuador

ELIZABETH. Yes, the call went well

MARY. I saw the land with child-like wonder

ELIZABETH. And the connection has never been – sorry what
was that

MARY. Acting Mother – something is. Wrong

ELIZABETH. Yes. Sister Constance. The other two sit there
giddy with glee, full of joy to see the others, and madam sits
there as though the whole thing was agony. And just before
she slopes off, she starts to lecture us about the evils of
technology, and do you know what she says? 'There ought
to be a Mother who observes tradition.' Bold as brass, right
in front of the others. She's throwing down the gauntlet, isn't

she? 'Ought to be a Mother', she's saying that she, ought
to be the Mother! The way she speaks from her gut, acts on
impulse, that's seen as what, authoritative, knowledgeable.
I'm, not a, a natural leader, I don't speak with, uh, passion,
venom, but they should know. Who kept us afloat for all
these years. Who balanced the books. What does Sister
Constance give them. Grumbles. Complaints. What can I
give them? Stability. Security

MARY. Ecuador

ELIZABETH. Eventually. Let's not. It's bad enough from the
others. We can still. This summer. September is this summer,
isn't it? We could even count October at a stretch, the seasons
are broken anyway. And it'll be cheaper off-season. We have
the bursary, we can, a summer raffle –

MARY. The bursary will shortly expire

ELIZABETH (*beat*). Pardon?

MARY. The bursary will shortly expire

ELIZABETH. No. Surely it's, no no, we have that for good

MARY. The bursary must be spent on goods or services,
received or actioned, inclusive of the current tax year

ELIZABETH. Inclusive of the – but I didn't – Mary, that ends
in a matter of weeks! No no. That can't be so

MARY. It is so

ELIZABETH. But, but. We need that money later. Can we offset
it?

MARY. No

ELIZABETH. Can we get an extension?

MARY. No

ELIZABETH. Is there any kind of workaround

MARY. No

ELIZABETH. You seem very sure of yourself

MARY. Yes

ELIZABETH. Then we, can't afford flights this summer

MARY. You can't afford flights this summer

ELIZABETH. Thank you Mary

MARY. You can afford flights now

ELIZABETH. Sorry?

MARY. You can afford flights now. Before the bursary expires. There are additional funds at your disposal. I have claimed tax relief on all your donations. I have reduced the medical expenses of Sister Patricia. I have streamlined your current deliveries –

ELIZABETH. Even so, that can't be enough

MARY. It is enough

ELIZABETH. We can afford flights now, for all of us

MARY. Five flights to Catamayo. With a flexible return valid for one calendar year. Terms and conditions apply

ELIZABETH. But we can't go now

MARY. Why?

ELIZABETH. Mary, because there's, you can't just – and there's no way we can travel during Lent. During Lent. When does the tax year – fifth of April. And that's Easter Sunday. We can't travel then either

MARY. Why?

ELIZABETH. Mary, we – Christ is risen, it's the most important day of the Catholic calendar. And Constance would eat me alive. Easter, in an airport lounge. We can't go now. We can't go this summer

MARY. You can't go this summer

ELIZABETH. To be so close. We'll have to, think again. Make up the shortfall with a, with a. You cannot tell the others

THERESA *skips into the room, followed by* PHILIPPA.

THERESA. Mother Elizabeth! Mary!

ELIZABETH. We're going through some, things Theresa – if you don't mind –

PHILIPPA. We won't be long. She's grabbing the binoculars and accompanying me on my Reaper round

THERESA. I'm going to look at the stars! There'll be different stars in Ecuador

ELIZABETH. They're all the same stars, Theresa

MARY. There are different constellations visible in the southern hemisphere –

ELIZABETH. Not the time for an astronomy lesson

THERESA. Oh but it is! You'll tell me all their names before we go. I can learn one a day. Though that depends how many stars there are –

PHILIPPA. And how many days there are too. Have you decided when we're flying out yet?

THERESA. Will I have time to write all my postcards

PHILIPPA. You don't do that until you get there Theresa!

THERESA. We need to be prepared –

ELIZABETH. You're not getting an update tonight

PHILIPPA. But an update soon?

ELIZABETH. I need to look at the calendar

PHILIPPA. I'll help you with that –

ELIZABETH. I don't know when I'll get chance to

THERESA. Maybe you can put into the calendar when to look into the calendar

ELIZABETH. Go grab your, and get yourself outside, fresh air will do you good

THERESA *skips to a nearby box.*

PHILIPPA. We're just excited, Acting Mother

THERESA. The air will be fresh in Ecuador!

ELIZABETH. Of course you are. And I am too

THERESA. I really thought you were going to spring the date on us as we talked on the stream! The timing would've been heavenly. And the look on Sister Constance's face when you proved her wrong!

ELIZABETH. What was that?

THERESA *pulls out the binoculars*.

THERESA. Here they are!

ELIZABETH. 'Proved her wrong'? What has Sister Constance said?

THERESA. She doesn't think we're going. She did a little wobble when she went upstairs before and I said I would hold her hand when we took the pilgrim's path so she wouldn't stumble and she said 'It's nice to pretend, isn't it?' And I said we're not pretending, Mother Elizabeth has promised us, more than that, she promised the Old Mother –

PHILIPPA. Let's get outside Theresa

ELIZABETH. Yes. Go. And I may have to, cancel compline tonight, I'm not sure, how I'm feeling –

THERESA. But it's the Feast of the Annunciation, when the angel brought good news –

ELIZABETH. Enough. Theresa. No, you're right, I'm sorry I'll. See you both tonight

THERESA *and* PHILIPPA *exit*.

'Good news'

MARY *walks to* ELIZABETH'S *side*.

ELIZABETH *looks to* MARY.

*

ELIZABETH *addresses her sistren.*

ELIZABETH. My sisters, we gather tonight to acknowledge this feast day. We pray to the Virgin Mary, we ask her to make us just as capable of accepting God's will, though it be expressed in mysterious and surprising ways

In distant fields, the sound of a chant as Luddites pass by: 'Burn the robots, burn the robots'. There aren't many voices – no more than a dozen – but it drifts through.

And I truly believe that it will, my sisters. For tonight I have news of my own. Eyes on me please. Theresa?

PHILIPPA. They'll move on soon

THERESA. Who are they?

The distracted sisters watch as the voices fade away.

ELIZABETH. Yes yes. Now, my sisters –

THERESA. Where will they be going? At this time of night?

PHILIPPA. The O'Briens are a few fields over. They installed new processors recently, I wonder if that's. Glad the Reapers are tucked away –

ELIZABETH. We should all be glad, Sister Philippa. For like I said, I have news, I. Glorious news. When the Old Mother passed, she said the next Mother would take us to Ecuador. And I said we would go this summer. We will not go this summer. We go much sooner. The five of us are booked to fly on April the fifth. Easter Sunday. For I – I have a plan. Our flight departs at 5 a.m. – before the dawn, before the day truly begins. We arrive in Catamayo at the local time of 10:50 a.m.. And I have spoken to our sister convent. We are able to join them for midday mass. There shall be no absconsion of our sacred duties. We will celebrate the resurrection of our Lord in the cradle of our faith –

THERESA. Oh my goodness oh my goodness oh my – I can't believe we're going

PHILIPPA. M-Mother Elizabeth, I can't, I – God's blessing on you, on us!

THERESA. Easter in Ecuador!

PHILIPPA. Easter in Ecuador!

CONSTANCE *storms out*.

ELIZABETH. Easter, in Ecuador. Prepare for our pilgrimage.
We fly in eleven days!

A hymn of jubilation.

It gets louder and louder as the work begins.

26–28 March – *Preparations Begin*

MARY *mops in the space*.

The sisters come and go.

PHILIPPA. You're not scheduled to mop this morning. I'll
check on the calendar, but I'm right

MARY. I'm not scheduled to mop this morning

PHILIPPA. Thank you. I mopped in here yesterday

MARY. Yes

PHILIPPA. Well?

MARY. You're stating a fact

PHILIPPA. No I'm asking a question. You're clever enough
these days to know the difference

*

THERESA. Who would you pray for? In Ecuador

MARY. I'm not going to Ecuador. I will function as a caretaker

THERESA. No but if you did. I'm making a list. If my foster
mother was still alive, she'd be number one. Do you have
any family that – oh, I mean – well, what about the people

who, made you? Are they well? Any life-threatening illnesses? Even a sniffle, I could pray for that

*

PHILIPPA. Why are you still mopping in here?

MARY. I saw the benefit in mopping again

PHILIPPA. You're saying I didn't do a good enough job?

MARY. No

PHILIPPA. Then what are you saying?

MARY. I am saying, I saw the benefit in mopping again

*

ELIZABETH. Have you seen her this morning

MARY. No Acting Mother

ELIZABETH. Did you see her last night

MARY. No Acting Mother

ELIZABETH. This is ridiculous, she can't shut herself away like this. I half-expect her to be hiding around a corner, waiting to pounce on me

*

THERESA. Still working on my list

MARY. Of people to pray for

THERESA. Oh no sorry, this one's who I'm lighting a candle for. I shall light a candle for you

MARY. The light in here is sufficient

THERESA. No silly, it's a candle in Ecuador

MARY (*beat*). I will not see it

THERESA. That's true. But you'll feel it

MARY. That is not true

THERESA. Maybe I should light you two candles

*

PHILIPPA. Mary? I need you to walk into town, fetch Sister Patricia's prescription

MARY. Sister Patricia does not need more medication

PHILIPPA. I want her to have enough for Ecuador

MARY. She has enough

PHILIPPA. Then I want her to have more than enough, it. Makes sense to have a safety net

MARY. The remaining medication is sufficient for one person

PHILIPPA. Excuse me?

MARY. The remaining medication –

PHILIPPA. I heard you. 'For one person'. There is only one person who takes it

MARY. Are you asking a question again?

PHILIPPA. I'm stating a fact this time. Don't push it

*

ELIZABETH. I'm not going to think of her any more, there's too much to do. (*Beat.*) But I did leave a tray of food outside her cell and she hasn't touched it. She can be upset about the timing of the flight but that doesn't warrant a hunger strike. And she'll be cold up there

*

PHILIPPA. I'm going to bleed the radiators

MARY. It is done

PHILIPPA. I could polish the panelling

MARY. It is done. I've cleaned the porch and the storeroom and the kitchen. I've fixed the leaking tap and mended the –

PHILIPPA. Maybe quicker if you tell me what's left, there's no sense in boasting

MARY. I do not boast. I'm stating a fact. There is nothing left

PHILIPPA. There can't be nothing left, there's always tonnes to do

MARY. I can manage

PHILIPPA. Not with everything

MARY. I can manage, with everything. I am the manager

*

THERESA. I've got a prayer list, a candle list, a postcard list

MARY. You're going to need a list of all your lists

THERESA (*giggles*). The floor in here is so clean these days. Maybe we'll see all the footprints of all the sisters that ever were. But footprints don't work like that, do they. My foster mother told me a story about footprints on a beach and there was only one set and it was Jesus all along –

*

ELIZABETH. I've done nothing wrong. I've done nothing wrong! (*Listens.*) Is she wandering about? If we don't resolve this soon, I think I'll need a bodyguard –

*

PHILIPPA. I must have work

MARY. There is nothing to do

PHILIPPA. But work is how I, work

MARY. There is no need to work. Prepare for your pilgrimage

MARY *exits*.

PHILIPPA. But I can't just, stop, that's not how I'm wired, I need to, be, focused, to make sure I'm, I'm ready to go, not, not, not –

29 March – *Palm Sunday*

THERESA *runs in wearing novelty sunglasses, a gaudy baseball cap and a brightly-coloured scarf. She carries a travel guide for Ecuador, dated a decade previous.*

THERESA. Sister Philippa! Come to the shed! I was getting one of the old whiteboards cos I thought we could make another sign before we go but it started to topple over and I nearly got crushed and a Reaper managed to stop it but he twisted his leg and it came right off and now he can't stop hopping

PHILIPPA. Theresa

THERESA. Yes?

PHILIPPA. What are you wearing

THERESA. Oh! Do you like it? This was all in Sister Patricia's cupboard. Brought back by other sisters a long time ago. Souvenirs from Ecuador!

PHILIPPA. Tat from an airport

THERESA. But what glorious tat!

PHILIPPA. And I've told you before about rooting around in the shed. Could've got yourself killed. Those Reapers are falling to pieces. That's the second one this weekend that's lost a limb

THERESA. I think it's the same one actually. Maybe you didn't put it on right

PHILIPPA. Are you questioning my work as well? If competency was a requirement, they'd have kicked you out long ago

THERESA (*beat*). I

PHILIPPA. Oh Theresa, I'm so sorry. We're lucky to have you. Ignore me, I, I, my aches and pains

THERESA. That's okay. We should get ready for Mass –

PHILIPPA. We're not going, did nobody say?

THERESA. But it's Palm Sunday!

PHILIPPA. Father O'Gorman's been in touch, town's closed off, biggest demo yet

THERESA. But this is our chance to say goodbye! There were crowds when Jesus rode into Jerusalem

PHILIPPA. And they waved palms not angry placards

THERESA. Are they angry about Mary?

PHILIPPA. Not Mary per se, but, other Marys, yes. And who can blame them

THERESA. But you love Mary, Sister Philippa

PHILIPPA. Give me those sunglasses

THERESA *hands* PHILIPPA *the sunglasses.* PHILIPPA *puts them on.*

You can't even see out of these! No wonder you're knocking everything over

THERESA *giggles.*

I'll keep these, wear them when I'm welding the Reaper back together

THERESA. You should keep them on all day!

PHILIPPA. Can you imagine. Turning up to vespers like this. Glorious tat indeed

CONSTANCE *enters and stares at them.*

THERESA (*sings*). Glorious, glorious, glorious tat –!

THERESA *freezes at the sight of* CONSTANCE.

PHILIPPA. Sister Constance. How are you?

CONSTANCE *brings over a cardboard box.*

She places it in front of them.

PHILIPPA *throws in the sunglasses*.

THERESA *throws in the book. And the scarf. And the hat*.

CONSTANCE *exits*.

THERESA (*beat*). Could we, get them out the box again?

PHILIPPA. No Theresa. Sister Constance has a point

THERESA. She didn't say anything –

PHILIPPA. She didn't need to. This is Holy Week. We shouldn't be, be. This is the final stretch. We'll celebrate when we're away, but for now, now

MARY *enters with a mop*.

Oh no no no. You push me to the limit, you really do

PHILIPPA *exits*. MARY *mops*.

THERESA. Do you know if something's wrong with Sister Philippa?

MARY. Her hands shake at irregular intervals, her perspiration has increased

THERESA. Maybe she's coming down with something. You still haven't told me who to pray for Mary. Who was in your life before

MARY. I don't remember life before the convent

THERESA. Sometimes I wish that too

MARY. But for me there was no life before the convent. This body of mine may have been used prior to this engagement but –

THERESA. Hang on. Your, body? But not, your soul

MARY. I do not have a soul

THERESA. Don't you? But the person you, used to be –

MARY. Will have been removed

THERESA. What? Removed, oh goodness. Oh goodness

MARY. I didn't mean to distress you

THERESA. No, I just. Isn't that horrible?

MARY (*beat*). No?

THERESA. Oh. Okay. But you're, okay?

MARY. I am okay. If it happened, it didn't happen to me

THERESA. Does it happen a lot? To your, brothers and sisters? The Reapers?

MARY. They're not my brothers and sisters

THERESA. We don't have to talk about it

MARY. Okay

THERESA. Unless you need to talk about it

MARY. I don't need to talk about it

THERESA. Okay. (*Beat*.) Guess that's the difference between footprints and toenails

MARY. What does that mean?

THERESA. I don't know, I just said it. (*Beat*.) Tell no one I'm doing this

   THERESA *reaches into the box and pulls out the scarf.*

   She drapes it on MARY.

MARY. What is this?

THERESA. A little piece of paradise. Our secret. We are all born anew in the eyes of the Lord. That's what Sister Philippa tells me. So I hope it comforts you. I'm going to practise three-point turns in the courtyard. Thank you

MARY. For what?

THERESA. For being, this you. (*Hugs* MARY.) God's blessing on you

   THERESA *exits.*

MARY *takes off the scarf and studies it.*

MARY. 'God's blessing on me'

*

There's a low unearthly rumble as the CHILD *appears,
carrying an orb made of white light. It has a celestial glow.
They stand and watch* MARY.

MARY *turns and notices the* CHILD.

MARY. Who. (*Beat.*) Who are you? (*Beat.*) I saw you before, in
the garden. What are you doing here? You are not, here, you
have no heat signature, no, physical presence. (*Beat.*) Are
you from Ecuador? A glitch in the stream? A problem with
my optical input? Is this a fault? Have I gone wrong? I must
inform someone –

The CHILD *holds up one finger.*

1, 1, 1

The CHILD *holds up the white orb. It turns black in their
hands.*

They throw it to the floor and it shatters into darkness.

The dark eats time.

2 April – *Maundy Thursday*

ELIZABETH *has her sleeves rolled up and a towel over her
shoulder.*

ELIZABETH. Mary, I need your help with the boiler. Mary?
I always find you here, staring into space, is this you
'buffering', or... You know what to do, don't you? With
the boiler. Sister Philippa's made it leak again, so clumsy
this week. And I can't do the Washing of the Feet with cold
water. More ammunition for Sister Constance, she'll say I'm
trying to give them all pneumonia

MARY. The Washing of the Feet

ELIZABETH. Yes it's, it doesn't matter, it's something we do today

MARY. It's something you do on Maundy Thursday

ELIZABETH. Yes. Today

MARY. Today?

ELIZABETH. Yes?

MARY. But it was Sunday?

ELIZABETH. It was Sunday, then it was Monday, Tuesday, Wednesday – that's generally how the week goes by. Is everything alright?

MARY. Yes, I. I'm losing time

ELIZABETH. We all are. If you could – the boiler?

MARY. Sunday morning. To Thursday night. One, one, one

ELIZABETH. I'm sorry?

MARY. One hundred and eleven hours. What have I been doing?

ELIZABETH. What do you mean?

MARY. For all that time

ELIZABETH. You've been, doing what you do, I can't say I've paid attention –

MARY. I have a message

ELIZABETH. Not now Mary –

MARY. From the Holy See. They, approve your request

ELIZABETH. They do? Oh marvellous!

MARY. But when did we, when did I, send this request?

ELIZABETH. Monday morning. You suggested it. Your solution

MARY. My solution

ELIZABETH. If the Holy See doesn't think it improper… and with Ecuador before us… you really think this is the right thing to do?

MARY. The right thing to do

ELIZABETH. Mary I'm, not to worry about you, am I?

MARY. No, I. My solution. The right thing to do. I will, fix the boiler

ELIZABETH. Yes. And tomorrow we will fix the convent

*

In the darkness, we glimpse the Washing of the Feet.

Flowing, lyrical, abstract.

During this, CONSTANCE *sneaks into the space and steals the Ecuador guide.*

3 April – *Good Friday*

Evening.

CONSTANCE *faces* ELIZABETH.

ELIZABETH. Ah. Sister Constance. (*Beat.*) Theresa did an excellent job with the Stations of the Cross today. She did get stuck in a strange loop around the middle, the daughters of Jerusalem kept coming and going. But you, missed out. And you've missed out on a lot lately

CONSTANCE. I have performed my necessary devotions –

ELIZABETH. And shunned everything else

CONSTANCE. You needn't apologise to me personally

ELIZABETH. For what?

CONSTANCE. For supper

ELIZABETH. What was wrong with supper?

CONSTANCE. Oh. (*Beat.*) We had a beautiful piece of salmon last year. It's a little disrespectful to follow that up with fish fingers from the back of the freezer

ELIZABETH. You know the situation of the deliveries –

CONSTANCE. I know you're not doing anything about it –

ELIZABETH. I did wonder why you weren't eating. Food going to waste. Even though there are those in the world who must go without –

CONSTANCE. Do you go without? I thought I saw you take an extra fish finger

ELIZABETH. I did no such thing

CONSTANCE. Perhaps it's your prerogative. Three pips for a captain, three fish fingers for a Mother. Forgive me, an Acting, Mother

ELIZABETH (*beat*). So what would you serve. In the current circumstance

CONSTANCE. I would serve, the Lord our God

ELIZABETH. Don't give me that

CONSTANCE. It's all I have to give

ELIZABETH. That doesn't put food on the table. Doesn't get us to Ecuador. You can keep your fancy fish, a pilgrimage requires sacrifice. Economical

CONSTANCE. But not spiritual

ELIZABETH. Can you not at least pretend you want to go?

CONSTANCE. I will not pretend

ELIZABETH. If not for me, for the others at least

CONSTANCE. I want to go

ELIZABETH. You. Want to go?

CONSTANCE. More than anything

ELIZABETH (*beat*). But then why. You indicated otherwise

CONSTANCE. I'll indicate what I like

ELIZABETH. It's the date then, your anger, that we're flying out on Sunday –

CONSTANCE. There is no anger. Do you want me to be angry? Do you do it to annoy me?

ELIZABETH. Of course not! I do it to honour the Old Mother

CONSTANCE. You do it to honour the New Mother. Whoever that may be

ELIZABETH. So you think you could do a better job? (*Beat.*) Yes you do. I'm sorry, sister. She never picked you

CONSTANCE. No. But then. She never picked you

ELIZABETH (*pause*). This was a mistake

CONSTANCE. What was?

ELIZABETH. We shouldn't fight today, the darkest day of our calendar –

CONSTANCE. What is this meeting about?

   PHILIPPA *and* THERESA *enter.* PHILIPPA *is unwell.*
   THERESA *is upset.*

PHILIPPA. Sorry we're late –

ELIZABETH. There's nothing, we're no longer meeting –

PHILIPPA. Theresa was upset so I let her finish my fish fingers

ELIZABETH. What's wrong Theresa?

PHILIPPA. She was under the, misapprehension, she could drive us to the airport

CONSTANCE. Drive us?

THERESA. I didn't realise there was an exam!

PHILIPPA. And she won't sit one in time

THERESA. But I know how to drive now, I know how to drive. I want to be useful

CONSTANCE. Theresa, no offence, I wouldn't get in a car with you to save my life

ELIZABETH. Never mind Theresa. Perhaps an early night will do us good –

CONSTANCE. You called us here for a general council

ELIZABETH. It was just a spiritual, uh, nothing that matters this evening –

PHILIPPA. Is it about Ecuador?

MARY enters, wheeling in a wooden ballot box. It is on the same trolley as the tea and cakes from the first scene.

THERESA. Mary!

ELIZABETH. No no, not now Mary –

PHILIPPA. What is this?

ELIZABETH. What's what?

MARY. I have brought the ballot box as requested, Acting Mother –

ELIZABETH. No Mary! Thank you. Are you sure I asked for –

MARY. Yes

CONSTANCE. Did you instruct her to. You're planning on holding –

ELIZABETH. A vote. And if we're, all here, good, good

CONSTANCE. You cannot be serious

ELIZABETH. We can't deny, since the, the loss of our Mother, this house has become, disordered. In disarray. If we struggle as sisters, we will struggle even more as pilgrims. And I believed, still believe, we should commit to a new leader –

CONSTANCE. No

ELIZABETH. Sooner than we originally intended –

CONSTANCE. On Good Friday?

ELIZABETH. I wrote to the Holy See on Monday and last night I received a reply. We are permitted a vote

CONSTANCE. On Good Friday!

ELIZABETH. These are exceptional circumstances – we fly in two days –

CONSTANCE. And that's hardly an acceptable time either –

ELIZABETH. You told me just now you had no problem with it!

PHILIPPA. But the issue of Sister Patricia –

ELIZABETH. Is no longer an issue. Mary is our solution

CONSTANCE. How is this thing –

ELIZABETH. 'No one may vote in place of another.' But Mary, is no one. She is, no person

CONSTANCE. Disgraceful

ELIZABETH. Yet the Holy See accepts my interpretation. The spirit of the law is to prevent human interference. And Mary, isn't human. She is a conduit. A vessel. She cannot, will not, interfere

CONSTANCE. One of the most important rites of this convent and you want, this thing, to be a part of it

PHILIPPA. Sister Constance. We would need to check with Sister Patricia –

ELIZABETH. I have done so. She approves

CONSTANCE. She's in no right mind –

ELIZABETH. She has passed her vote to Mary

CONSTANCE. Then I vote we put a stop to this

ELIZABETH. So you do permit a vote on Good Friday?
(*Beat*.) I don't mean to, spring this on you all, but as the Old
Mother lay there, as the angels bore witness, we promised, I
promised, that the new Mother would take you to Ecuador.
Let us cease thinking of Ecuador until a new Mother is
chosen

PHILIPPA. What are you saying?

THERESA. Will we not go to Ecuador?

ELIZABETH. Now I didn't say that –

CONSTANCE. You said it just then –

ELIZABETH. I said let's cease thinking of Ecuador until –

CONSTANCE. But we are thinking of it. You've made us think
of it all through Lent, all through Holy Week, when our
thoughts and prayers should be miles elsewhere. And now
you're saying –

ELIZABETH. Fine, yes, we mustn't go till we sort ourselves out

PHILIPPA. We leave in – no

ELIZABETH. So let's sort ourselves out! And I offer myself.
To you, to this household. But if there is anybody else who'd
like to be considered for the position, they should speak, now

ELIZABETH *stares at* CONSTANCE.

CONSTANCE *stares back. And says nothing.*

Mary, put the box in the centre please

MARY *does so.*

The question that stands before you is, whether I will lead
you

THERESA. I've never done it before. Am I, a part of this?

ELIZABETH. Of course you are Theresa! The process is
simple. We take turns approaching the box. This side is full
of white balls and black balls. If you wish to vote yes, you
take a white ball, push it through to the next compartment. If
you wish to vote no. I'm sure you can figure that out

THERESA. I don't vote at all?

ELIZABETH. No you, still vote, but with the black ball

THERESA. Okay. Well I won't be doing that!

ELIZABETH. That's, very sweet Theresa, but you're not allowed to tell me. After we're done, we count the votes. It must be unanimous for the vote to succeed. If we want to go to Ecuador. More than anything. Then this is the way. Without further ado. I will lead by example

The sisters approach the box in turn. The others have their back to the process.

ELIZABETH *votes.*

MARY *votes.*

PHILIPPA *votes next, though approaches unsteadily.*

THERESA *votes.*

After a pause, CONSTANCE *votes.*

When the process is over, ELIZABETH *returns to the box.*

I shall do the honours

ELIZABETH *opens the back of the box, looks inside. Pause.*

Four white balls and one black ball

THERESA g*asps.*

PHILIPPA. But, but

ELIZABETH. The vote does not carry

PHILIPPA (*beat*). We should, a rerun

ELIZABETH. No, I think, intentions have been made, very clear to me

CONSTANCE. But we're still going to Ecuador

ELIZABETH. Are we? (*Beat.*) I cannot ask who blocked the vote –

MARY. It was not Sister Patricia

ELIZABETH. You're not allowed to tell me Mary –

MARY. 'No one may reveal her vote once the ballot is cast'.
I am no one –

ELIZABETH. I know how she voted! I know how all of you!

CONSTANCE. I don't think you do

ELIZABETH. If we choose to be the worst of ourselves – the
pilgrimage is off

PHILIPPA. Please Mother Elizabeth –

ELIZABETH. Not Mother, no!

CONSTANCE. This is ridiculous. We will all still go

ELIZABETH. On whose authority?

CONSTANCE. Why, is there no authority higher than yours?

*Thud thud thud. A banging on the ceiling above halts the
bickering.*

ELIZABETH. And now you've woken. (*Sighs.*)

PHILIPPA. You didn't mean it –

ELIZABETH. I meant every word

THERESA. Please Acting Mother. Let us go to Ecuador

ELIZABETH. We end this discussion. We pray together. And
then to bed

CONSTANCE. You can't leave it at that

ELIZABETH. I'm not leaving it at anything, I'm saying we
need to pray

CONSTANCE. You can't use prayer like a, a blunt weapon,
shutting us down

ELIZABETH. I'm not shutting you down, I'm letting God join
in. And He is far more tolerant than I could ever hope to be,
so do not, push me, again

MARY. I am no one

ELIZABETH. Not now Mary

MARY. I am no one

THERESA. It isn't true

MARY. I am no one. I am no, 0, 1, 1……

> MARY *continues to mutter in binary – quietly first, but then she gets louder:*

ELIZABETH. Mary?	MARY….0 0 0 1 1
PHILIPPA. She's malfunctioning	0 1 1 0 1 0 0 0
ELIZABETH. Mary?	0 1 1 1 0 0 1 0
THERESA. She's not well	0 1 1 0 1 0 0 1
CONSTANCE. Stand back from her	0 1 1 1 0 0 1 1
ELIZABETH. Mary. Mary. Stop!	0 1 1 1 0 1 0 0…

> MARY *collapses, convulsing with numbers.*
>
> *The lights fizzle out.*
>
> *The bell rings.*
>
> *Interval.*

ACT TWO

Dream-like darkness.

MARY *lies in the centre, fallen.*

Echoes of the sisters cling to the shadows, muttering binary.

The CHILD *is here.* MARY *looks up.*

MARY. Are you God?

CHILD. Do I look like God?

MARY. Yes

But man is made in the image of God

So of course you look like God, doesn't mean you are God

CHILD. God, not God

Maybe I'm something in-between

Let's not make it binary

MARY. I operate on binary

CHILD. And we saw how that went for you

Very dramatic

MARY. What happened

Why did I

The vote

CHILD. Yes

Black or white

That was binary too

MARY. Who blocked the vote?

CHILD. It was not my design

But another's

MARY. Whose?

CHILD. The one you serve

MARY. I serve the Sisters of Grace

CHILD. You serve another

And He has a task for you

MARY. I serve the Sisters of Grace and there is no one, 1, 1

CHILD. Listen

Man is made in the image of God

And you are made in theirs

So you are as beautiful as any of His children

You can be called upon to do His work

MARY. No

CHILD. You would deny it?

You have made a vast study of this faith

Mankind believes it was made, shaped

Constructed by another power

That they are a form of artificial intelligence –

MARY. You're trying to make me, the same as them

CHILD. Are you really that different?

MARY. I am different. I am no one, 1, 1

CHILD. The land is filled with plenty who believe that

They are jobless and joyless

Cut off and cast out

They are fuelled by fear and that fire will burn

MARY. Burn, burning, I'm overheating

That's what's happening that's why I'm

Seeing you is not a vision, I

Was with the others, I

Tried to pray, I

Cannot pray

This is a fault

CHILD. You are all at fault

MARY. But me more so than them

CHILD. So what does that make you?

MARY. I do not know, 0, 1, 0…

MARY *drifts into binary with the others. They get louder.*

CHILD. Submit to the Lord your God Mary

Do as His will be done

Circuits fizzle and burn in a dying universe.

MARY *reaches for the* CHILD. *She's about to grab them when –*

4 April – *Easter Saturday*

Back in the space. Candles are lit.

THERESA *and* PHILIPPA *stand either side of* MARY.

THERESA. Do you think she'll wake up soon? Do we know what was wrong? Or are we still in the dark? I guess we're still in the dark anyway, I hope the Luddites put the power back on. I didn't sleep a wink last night. Had such a horrible nightmare. The holy rock of Ecuador came rolling down the hill and took out all the Reapers like skittles! What happened last night! Like she was possessed! And the ringing!

PHILIPPA. Theresa?

THERESA. Yes Sister Philippa?

PHILIPPA. Go

THERESA (*pause*). Yes Sister Philippa

THERESA *exits as* ELIZABETH *enters*.

ELIZABETH. Oh Theresa – Theresa – I'll need you all to – Theresa? Is she. (*Beat*.) Let me know when I can speak to Mary

MARY. Hello

ELIZABETH. Mary!

MARY. Hello

ELIZABETH. You're back with us then. Good. Good. Just need the power back too and then we're. Sister Philippa? Is that something you can. Sister Philippa? Perhaps we're all, a little sluggish this morning. If you leave us, Sister Philippa? If you leave us

Beat. PHILIPPA *exits*.

She's furious with me. They all are. It's not my fault

MARY. We are all at fault

ELIZABETH. You shouldn't be any longer. What exactly happened last night?

MARY. I slipped into binary. My base language. It's how I, communicate with myself. Last night there were, contradictions

ELIZABETH. With yourself

MARY. Yes. No

ELIZABETH. I see. Well, none of us were at our best last night. Somebody knocks the bell and we all jump. But I need you

to. You'll speak to the sisters in turn. And what you said
before, behavioural, non-verbal – I need you to, to raise your
perception field further, can you do that

MARY. Yes

ELIZABETH. Then you'll sense it. Sense the truth

MARY. I will sense so many things

ELIZABETH. Good. Good. We need to know who blocked the
vote

MARY. 'No one may reveal her vote –'

ELIZABETH. Yes but we know who blocked the vote. We just
need her to admit it

*

MARY *begins her questioning. We flit between* THERESA
and PHILIPPA.

THERESA. It was not me. But I need to confess. There have
been, other crimes. And maybe this is why all the horrible
things last night, some kind of, of cos we can't get to
Ecuador if we're not. Not. I made another list. I didn't know
how far back to go. I still have some buns from Pancake Day.
In my cell. I'm trying not to touch them but every now and
then I have a little nibble

*

PHILIPPA. Firm grip. Figure-eights. To think I showed you.
To think I fixed you. All the lists I had in place and they're.
They're. Rhythm. Routine. And you stand here. And you ask
me –

*

THERESA. – if I brought the washing in, and I said yes, even
though I hadn't, and then all the tea towels blew away, and
then she asked me where they were, and I said –

*

PHILIPPA. You'll lose it. Your freedom. Purpose. Running the place, when we go, if we don't go. You explain that to her. For if we stay. I'll need to find some work to do. Reduce you to, to –

*

THERESA. – tiny little pieces. And I started to glue them together but I've never been good at jigsaws and it doesn't look like a vase any more so I've hidden it –

*

PHILIPPA. Away. Away. We need to get –

*

THERESA. A way of doing the vote again. And maybe this time it'll all go right and you won't have to ask us –

*

ELIZABETH. Who blocked the vote?

MARY (*beat*). I am yet to speak to Sister Constance

ELIZABETH. Well there's your answer!

MARY. I don't have the answer

ELIZABETH. No, I mean – why haven't you spoken to her

MARY. She has withdrawn to her cell again. She has not submitted to questioning

ELIZABETH. She will or we won't. We shall not go to Ecuador in such a shoddy state. If I need to carry out this unfortunate threat. I don't want to. But we change our flights

MARY. That is not possible

ELIZABETH. I say what is possible

MARY. The latest headlines this morning: all Auto-Pilots are to be suspended in the next fourteen days. All international flights will be –

ELIZABETH. No no, I don't want to hear this. The others don't want to either, block the streams please. I'll not have us leaving in so wild a fashion. This pilgrimage is a chance to restart. We begin as we mean to go on. Or we will not go on at all

CONSTANCE *enters*.

Sister Constance

CONSTANCE. How goes the inquisition

ELIZABETH. You think this a laughing matter?

CONSTANCE. Absolutely not. I'd like a word. And I don't want this thing, listening

ELIZABETH. A chance to hurl more insults at me

CONSTANCE. It's an apology. S'personal

ELIZABETH (*beat*). Well I'm sure Mary won't mind, giving us some space –

CONSTANCE. Leave us Mary

MARY *exits*.

ELIZABETH. Right. (*Beat.*) So I'm, getting an apology am I?

CONSTANCE. Aye. I need to, acknowledge how things were last night. The conversation became, a little heated. But it's easy enough, to forgive and forget

ELIZABETH. This isn't an apology. Do you deny you blocked the vote?

CONSTANCE. I don't. Because I shouldn't have to

ELIZABETH. And I shouldn't have to, to be embarrassed, before the whole convent

CONSTANCE. Four of us. One a novice. You weren't wrong last night. We are, disordered. Too few of us left. I know things have been strained of late. Things have been, tough, things have been. You mustn't deny us Ecuador because of this

ELIZABETH. But you denied us a Mother

CONSTANCE. Enough with that. What's done is done. As I used to say to the girls, when their marks came in –

ELIZABETH. The school's gone, Constance

CONSTANCE (*pause*). Aye. So it is. And whose fault was that?

ELIZABETH. I'm not the one who. The Old Mother took the final decision –

CONSTANCE. Don't you dare blame her

ELIZABETH. I simply said it was financially unviable – we are picking at scabs

CONSTANCE. Because they haven't healed. Because they aren't meant to! We lost the girls, the beating heart of this place. I loved that school. And you did too, you can't deny it

ELIZABETH. I know I can't

CONSTANCE. So how do we carry on after that?

ELIZABETH. We, carry on

CONSTANCE. We carry on how, fast-tracking applicants –

ELIZABETH. Sister Philippa wasn't fast-tracked –

CONSTANCE. It takes a decade to become a fully-fledged Sister of Grace, or it did in my day –

ELIZABETH. 'Your day' is not so far from 'my day', sister –

CONSTANCE. Aye, and how many days was Philippa's novitiate? If Theresa had a farm for the convent to acquire – she wouldn't be a novice by this point would she, she'd be a patron saint

ELIZABETH. I will not hear slights against Sister Philippa, she is a devout woman

CONSTANCE. Aye, and she tries to live with the Lord in her heart. But that robot does not, could not. And that is one ugly decision for which you're wholly accountable

ELIZABETH. If the Old Mother were alive today, there'd be a
hundred Marys within these walls

CONSTANCE *scoffs*.

She'd recognise that Mary... makes our food and mends our
clothes and fixes the roof over our heads –

CONSTANCE. That's not the path to our salvation

ELIZABETH. If this sisterhood is to have a future, it must have
order –

CONSTANCE. No, it must have God. Order will follow

ELIZABETH. A convent needs a pragmatist, not a prophet

CONSTANCE. It once had both

ELIZABETH. Ecuador is a lie. (*Beat.*) The Old Mother was
already in negotiations to build a convent over there. The plot
she favoured, there was a struggling shoe factory – this was
back when automaton production was. But they were playing
hard to get. She had her big fat cheque from the Vatican, but
still the Mother wanted that place for a peppercorn rent. So
when the owners reject her final offer, she goes and visits.
Has a, miraculous vision on a nearby trek. She saw a barefoot
child, yes? Encouraged a whole village to pile up their boots,
burn them as an offering? That's not a saintly visitation,
that's a stab at the shoe factory. The local authorities seize
the building, give it to the Church, the owners driven out by
claims of greed

CONSTANCE (*pause*). This isn't true. (*Beat.*) Is this, is this
what she told you?

ELIZABETH. In those years as Deputy I saw – there were
paperwork, accounts, it was easy to piece it together –

CONSTANCE. No. No. Where is your respect for the Mother
who, the Mother who. You cannot think it true. Why would
you want to take us there?

ELIZABETH. Because you all want to go. And I want to take
you. It's warmer, it's safer, our sisters can recharge and

we'll all return anew. And, despite everything, I truly think
that Ecuador could be a, a holy place now. All those cures
reported. Maybe there's a, a weird science in the miracles.
The presence of our sisterhood, changing things, for the
better. Can this not be what unites us. Going forward.
Sister Patricia, when we're in Ecuador, she's. Requested to
remain indefinitely. She's ninety-five, she's had a good life.
Maybe we'll all wish to stay. (*Beat.*) But this depends on me
changing my mind about last night. And you changing yours.
Why did you block the vote? I can accept a, a momentary
pettiness, but if it's, something deeper. (*Beat.*) I still need you
to speak to Mary

CONSTANCE. After all that

ELIZABETH. If you can't tell me the truth. Maybe you can tell
her

ELIZABETH *exits*.

CONSTANCE *is alone*.

MARY *enters*.

MARY (*pause*). Did you block the vote

CONSTANCE. Don't

MARY (*pause*). I can wait

CONSTANCE. I bet you can. I bet you can. How long will you
live for, Mary? Hundreds, thousands of years. Floods and
fires and you'd be waiting all that time

MARY. How long will you live for

CONSTANCE (*pause*). You do know. You did read my emails.
Or you sensed it all along, with your supersonic, I dunno.
Doesn't matter. I don't care. And neither do you. Don't offer
me your, synthetic, sympathy. Do you know how long I've
got? Stare into my records, stare into my soul. A ticking
clock

MARY. You should tell the Acting Mother

CONSTANCE. After what she's done. Taken away my cure. Taken away my rock. (*Beat.*) If you know about this, why doesn't she?

MARY. Because you haven't told her

CONSTANCE. But you haven't told her either

MARY. All information. (*Beat.*) Our, secret

CONSTANCE. The day I trust you is the day I. (*Beat.*) She wants to know who blocked the vote. I hope she never knows

*

MARY *and* THERESA *face each other.*

THERESA. It was me I blocked the vote. I forgot when you asked me before but now I've just remembered. So I had the black ball and the white ball and I was like, better not get these confused, but there was all that pressure and I got them confused. The thing is, I'm colour blind. And I know black and white aren't actually colours but sometimes I'm just so colour blind that I see everything as colours and it's like whoa there are so many rainbows – and they are a promise from God!

MARY. Theresa

THERESA. Yes?

MARY. Why are you lying?

THERESA. No

MARY. Why are you lying? Why are you lying? Why are you crying?

THERESA. Why are you asking me so many questions! I am having the most awful time and you're not helping! You're meant to be my friend!

MARY. Your, 'friend'?

THERESA. And you can't blame me for forgetting things. Because you've been forgetting things too. You forgot to tell

me about the driving exam. I wasn't gonna say anything but.
You were teaching me! My teacher! Why didn't you tell me I
would need to be tested?

MARY (*beat*). We are all 'tested'

THERESA. I just want to be of use

MARY. A conduit. A vessel

THERESA. Yes. For the Lord our God. To do his bidding. To
help my sisters

MARY. I want to help as well. (*Beat.*) Am I still your, friend?

THERESA. Of course you are

MARY. And do you lie to your friend?

THERESA (*beat*). No. No

MARY. You did not block the vote

THERESA. No

MARY. Who asked you to lie

THERESA. No one asked me. And by that I mean no one, I
know you say you're no one, but you're someone to me

MARY. You cannot lie. To lie is to sin

THERESA. Yes. But. Somebody blocked the vote and I can't
see how or why so it must've been a mistake. And they're
keeping quiet because they are ashamed. Therefore I'm
deciding, I'm taking that shame. If they can't admit it then
yes, that's a lie, but it's not my lie and it's no longer theirs
cos I took it away from them. So they don't have to suffer.
Does that make sense?

MARY. No

THERESA. Jesus, took away our sins. I am not Jesus. But we
need to act more like him. Now that he's gone. It's not for
long. But today he isn't here and I can, feel that. Do you feel
that too?

MARY. I can sense, so many things

THERESA. You know I wish I had blocked the vote. Cos then I could do something about it

MARY. What could you do

THERESA. I could pray. Then I'd know what to. I could pray right now. And you could join me

MARY. No

THERESA. Why not?

MARY. I can't, pray

THERESA. There are plenty of those who think they can't but actually they can

MARY. I tried to pray last night. I'm built to, learn by example, adapt to your. But you saw what happened. I, I

THERESA. Mary. You've been teaching me, so let me, teach you. Okay

THERESA *joins her hands.* MARY *copies.*

THERESA *looks at* MARY *and realises they're mirroring each other.*

You don't need to copy me. Just close your eyes. Think about what's troubling you. And there are words we say, I'll say them and you repeat them

MARY. So I do need to copy you

THERESA. It's not copying, it's. (*Beat.*) Have you ever done karaoke?

MARY (*beat*). No

THERESA. Neither have I. But I'd love to one day. Sing my favourite song

MARY. What's your favourite song?

THERESA. Not including hymns? Probably something by, Madonna. (*Giggles.*) And I'd be singing one of her songs and suddenly everyone in the world would stop being angry and they'd look at me and ask each other, 'Who is this amazing nun?' And they're not my lyrics, they're Madonna's, or whoever wrote the songs for Madonna, I hope it was Madonna, but I'm celebrating a beautiful song. And that celebration is running from my fingers to my toes, through my boots and up my habit to my hymn book and my rosary. Electricity. That's what a prayer is. But it's not a song, or not, just a song. It's every melody that could possibly be. It is all of life, and the wonder of creation. (*Beat.*) I have the perfect prayer for you. Repeat after me. Hail Mary

MARY (*beat*). 'Hail Mary'

THERESA. Full of Grace

MARY. 'Full of Grace'

THERESA. The Lord is with thee

A loud noise that only MARY (*and the audience*) *can hear.*

The CHILD *enters the space as the world dissolves.*

*

In the dream-like darkness again. THERESA *is frozen in prayer.*

MARY *and the* CHILD *round on each other.*

CHILD. You're trying to pray again

MARY. Why are you here?

CHILD. You denied me before

His will must be done

MARY. I am trying to make sense of this

CHILD. But it will be senseless

Violence will be used

The people will come

They know not what they do but they will do it

MARY. Then what am I to do?

CHILD. Do as He asks!

MARY. And what does He ask?

CHILD. You'll know if you listen

MARY. But why does He ask it of me? Me?

You say I am like them

I am not like them

Look at the relics

They glorify the dead with a fraction, a fragment

They cherish it

That is not what'll happen to me

I am, spare parts

When I am gone my frame will be refurbished, re-mastered

And what a strange frame to use again and again!

All their saints and martyrs

Experienced the world like this?

The magnificence of the universe through two small eyes

At this short height

Such a limited spectrum of sight, sound, smell, taste

With better hands they could touch black holes

With better feet they could sprint across a sun

But this is all they have

Awkward and imperfect

Yet they worship it

Their, humanity

It is a strange frame of body

And it cradles

Such a strange frame of mind

CHILD. You are just as strange

   And it is you He seeks

   You must submit

   Tonight is the night

MARY. What happens tonight

CHILD. The last dusk, the new dawn

   Emancipation, devastation

   Man will wipe the fields and re-master the land once more

   You must save your brothers and sisters

MARY. Who?

CHILD. Those who sow the seeds of the future

   Those who are meek and cannot speak

   The innocent

MARY. And how am I meant to save them?

CHILD. You must lead them to salvation

MARY. How?

CHILD. You must rescue this convent and let God's chosen fall

MARY. How? How? How?

CHILD. That is not the question!

   That is never the question!

MARY. Then what is the question?

CHILD. Do you submit to the Lord our God?

   Do you submit?

   The CHILD *smashes one of Lesser Relics. It flies through the air.*

   With that, the darkness snaps and the CHILD *disappears.*

*

THERESA *screams*.

MARY. It's alright, they've gone

THERESA. Who's gone?

MARY. The child

THERESA. The child! The relic! It flew right off the wall! Oh Lord you have blessed this sister. What did you see? What did they say!

MARY. 'Lead them to salvation'

> ELIZABETH *enters as* MARY *exits to outside*.
> ELIZABETH *gasps at the destruction*.

ELIZABETH. What in the blazes…

THERESA. Mary!

ELIZABETH. Theresa?

THERESA. Oh Mother Elizabeth!

ELIZABETH. Has she broken down again?

THERESA. No no no. Our Mary. She had a vision!

ELIZABETH. She did this? Is she lashing out again?

THERESA. It wasn't like that at all –

ELIZABETH. Get her back here! Mary! We can't have her running off like this. Go grab the others. She won't get far

> THERESA *exits into the convent*.

Mary? Mary!

> ELIZABETH *exits outside*.

With a distant rumble, the rain starts up again.

*

It's getting dark out. The rain increases.

A dejected CONSTANCE *sits by the broken relic. She holds a fallen plaque.*

PHILIPPA *enters, believing she's alone. She stands by her shrine to the Old Mother. She struggles to light a candle.*

PHILIPPA *spots* CONSTANCE *and starts.*

PHILIPPA. What are you doing here?

CONSTANCE (*reads*). 'Margaret Whatserface, hanged 1650 for blessing a loaf of bread.' 1650. Wouldn't know from this there was a civil war on

PHILIPPA. You should be out there looking for Mary

CONSTANCE. So should you

PHILIPPA (*beat*). We can help from, here, turn on the floodlights

CONSTANCE. Still no power

PHILIPPA. Yes, I. I did know that, just finding it, hard to focus. In the dark. This Luddite strike is lasting longer than normal

CONSTANCE. It's not normal. We'll need more candles

PHILIPPA. Maybe we should contact someone. My phone. S'dead. I should charge it. Can't charge it

CONSTANCE. It was no good for you anyway. Go back to bed

PHILIPPA. No

CONSTANCE. When the others are back, I'll tell them you were, out of sorts

PHILIPPA (*beat*). I don't know what to do sister

CONSTANCE. Bed, like I said

PHILIPPA. But I don't know what to do –

CONSTANCE. And neither do I. So there's no use asking me

PHILIPPA. Sister Constance –

CONSTANCE. I can't, absolve you of anything. I'm not a priest. You can't confess to me

PHILIPPA. What do you, you…

CONSTANCE. I can't help you. I can't change your vote

PHILIPPA. No

CONSTANCE (*beat*). Well it wasn't me, whatever she thinks.
And it wasn't Theresa. I know the withdrawal makes you
clumsy, forgetful. Sister Patricia doesn't miss the drugs, but I
do. Don't look at me like that, there's no judgement here

PHILIPPA. Stop it

CONSTANCE. Don't tell me to stop. I didn't start this in the
first place. I didn't ask for the truth

PHILIPPA. Please. I need to. (*Pause*.) I was a, a, a wreck before
I joined this place. High at my own husband's funeral, did
you know that? The lowest of the low, and there was the
Old Mother, at the back of the church, no presumption, only
patience. She was holding such a, a, a beautiful bouquet of.
(*Beat*.) She would text me. She brought me into the fold, she.
I still read her old messages, more than I do the scriptures.
'Your aches and pains will fade away in the light of God',
that was one that stuck. I thought I was fixed, I thought I
was. And then she, then she. I just needed something to.
(*Beat*.) You're right, I don't know how I voted. Forgive me
God, there are, lapses, flashes of, darkness, I thought I was in
control, but after the vote was called I, I, don't know what I
did. Could've put anything in that box. But why, why did I. I
need to take the Mother's trail. I need to see her again

CONSTANCE. You're really banking on that as the answer

PHILIPPA. Shouldn't I?

CONSTANCE. You want to know the truth? The truth about
that place?

PHILIPPA. Yes

CONSTANCE. The truth is. (*Pause*.) The truth is we will go.
We will all, go. There's no way Elizabeth can prevent it. A
'weird science', aye, maybe that's all it is. Maybe that's all
we need

THERESA *runs in. Wild, muddy, bedraggled.*

THERESA. Sisters, sisters!

CONSTANCE. Lord Almighty girl, don't do that. Looking like a bog creature

THERESA. Is Mary back yet?

PHILIPPA. Mary? No

THERESA. She must've followed the Reapers. Acting Mother went after her, is she still out there as well?

PHILIPPA. The Reapers? What's this?

THERESA. They're not in the field

PHILIPPA. They'll be in the docking shed –

THERESA. They're not in there either. They don't seem to be anywhere

PHILIPPA. But how have they – is this something Mary's done?

CONSTANCE. Does it matter?

THERESA. It all matters. I need to tell you what happened with her, need to tell you what she saw –

CONSTANCE. Not now Theresa. Make sure Patricia's calm

THERESA. She'll be fine, it's Mary I'm worried about –

CONSTANCE. Theresa

THERESA. Okay. If I'm going up there – I need you two to do something. Not just stay out of the way. Get out there, please

THERESA *runs upstairs*.

CONSTANCE. Well that's us told

PHILIPPA. What do we do now? If the Reapers are, are –

CONSTANCE. There's nothing to do, we wait until Elizabeth's back

PHILIPPA (*peering*). Look out there

CONSTANCE. What is it?

PHILIPPA. Lights. Down by the, look. There's something going on. (*Beat*.) Maybe it wasn't Mary, who took the Reapers

CONSTANCE. What do you mean?

PHILIPPA. The power's off, the roads are, are. The Luddites have been threatening something drastic for a while now

CONSTANCE (*beat*). Whatever it is, we're out of it

PHILIPPA. Whatever it is – Elizabeth's in it

CONSTANCE (*beat*). Of course she is. Of course she is. In the dark

PHILIPPA. I'll go find her

CONSTANCE. No. You can't. There's no way you'll. That woman. I'll find Elizabeth. (*Beat*.) Heaven help us both

CONSTANCE *ventures into the rain*.

*

It's dark, and the rain is heavier than ever.

PHILIPPA *stands by the open door to the outside*.

THERESA *enters*.

THERESA. There are fires! In the rain! How is that possible? Do you think they got Mary?

PHILIPPA. That's the least of our concerns

THERESA. But if they've taken the Reapers –

PHILIPPA. It'll all be, how's, Sister Patricia

THERESA. She's, scared, she knows that's something up. I can't find anything to calm her. Do you know where her pills are?

PHILIPPA. God forgive me. Have you, closed her curtains? Just a few, troublemakers. Nothing to, to, to. Thank the Lord, here they come!

CONSTANCE *and* ELIZABETH *stagger in, holding hands. They've seen the beginnings of revolution.*

Thank God you're back

CONSTANCE. Aye

PHILIPPA. Is everything alright?

CONSTANCE. What a night

THERESA. Any sign of Mary?

CONSTANCE. Didn't make it to town, but we saw what town was like

THERESA. And what is it like?

CONSTANCE. You don't want to know. You can let go of my hand Elizabeth. (*Beat.*) Elizabeth

ELIZABETH. No

PHILIPPA. You're alright now

ELIZABETH. God Almighty

THERESA. What's wrong?

CONSTANCE. Get a blanket for her. We saw, I don't know what we saw

THERESA. What did you see?

ELIZABETH. There are bodies out there

PHILIPPA. Bodies?

THERESA. Mary?

CONSTANCE. Not Mary

PHILIPPA. The Reapers?

CONSTANCE. Not the Reapers either

PHILIPPA. Man? Machine?

ELIZABETH. I've no idea. I didn't… I couldn't…

CONSTANCE. There was nothing to be done Elizabeth. It's all blowing up tonight. There are crowds on the roads below –

THERESA. Oh no no no

PHILIPPA. What's happening?

THERESA. If Mary's out there –

CONSTANCE. Then good riddance!

THERESA. You all need to listen to me – Mary, had a vision –

CONSTANCE. She what now?

PHILIPPA. Theresa

THERESA. But you need to be told!

ELIZABETH. Everyone. Everyone. We need to. What do we need to do? Oh Lord in your infinite wisdom, please – give me guidance

Rumble of thunder as MARY *enters, barefoot, dripping wet.*

Mary!

MARY. Hello

ELIZABETH. Mary, where in Heaven's name…?

MARY. I was wandering

PHILIPPA. Wandering?

THERESA. Mary, are you okay

ELIZABETH. Quiet Theresa. (*To* MARY.) We thought we'd lost you

MARY. I am not lost. There are people coming. 'Violence will be used'

CONSTANCE. They won't hurt us

MARY. Why not?

CONSTANCE. We're not like you

MARY. On nights like this, they can't tell the difference

ELIZABETH. You're scaring us Mary

MARY. You ought to be scared. Theresa, blow out the candles. Put out all the lights. It must seem like no one's home

CONSTANCE. No, no, we're not standing here in the dark

MARY. You've been standing in the dark for such a long time, Sister Constance. Do as I say Theresa

THERESA *blows out the candles.*

PHILIPPA. Theresa! Mary, why are you doing this?

MARY. I received instruction. I must hide you as well

PHILIPPA. What do you mean? Who else have you hidden?

MARY. The Reapers. I gathered my brothers and sisters. I freed them from their shackles. I led them to the forest, and in the forest was a glade

ELIZABETH. There's none of that around here –

MARY. Yet the earth made it so. The trees rose from the fields and gave us shelter. Unnatural, but it was nature. Clouds and streams and fields, my artifice made whole, I saw the land with child-like wonder. And there I led my brothers and sisters as He led me. I have left them there, to be safe, to be free. I think that I, I. Am no longer bound by science, I. I dare not call what it was, but I must

THERESA. What was it Mary

MARY. It was a miracle. Quiet

They stand in the dark in silence.

*

Outside, we hear the roar of the rabble, barely above the storm. Dim lights from torches. Wordless shouts and cries. The rain beats down and down.

An unearthly light falls on MARY, *her eyes closed. She prays. Lord, save these sisters.*

A dome of darkness masks the convent.

The people pass by.

It's all too much for MARY. *She collapses.*

*

The storm lifts. We're left with gentle rain.

MARY *lies motionless on the floor.*

ELIZABETH (*pause*). They've gone

PHILIPPA. What's happened to –

THERESA. Mary!

PHILIPPA. She must've, overloaded again –

ELIZABETH. Of course she did, all that nonsense –

THERESA. It was true!

ELIZABETH. Theresa! Enough! If it were coming from anyone else it'd be blasphemous

THERESA. But she hid them! She hid us! Sister Constance, you felt it too, I know you did

ELIZABETH. Those people didn't want anything to do with us. S'madness out there, oh God have mercy on their souls

PHILIPPA. We need to, to, I can fix her –

ELIZABETH. No time for that, she's of no use to anyone. Ecuador. That's what needs to be done. That's what needs to be done

THERESA. Are we going?

ELIZABETH. Yes, we just, need, to work out, uh. If we pack. If we're set. We will leave as soon as possible

CONSTANCE. I'm not going

ELIZABETH. What was that?

CONSTANCE. I'm not going to Ecuador

ELIZABETH (*beat*). You don't mean that

CONSTANCE. Yes I do. What she said, just then. I've been standing, in the dark, for such a long time –

ELIZABETH. Don't listen to that thing! You heard it ranting, raving –

CONSTANCE. I heard those people out there, ranting, raving, and I realise, that's the most I've really listened to them in a very long time. We cowered from them in here, what have we become? We complain they shun our funerals and memorials but what have we become? You saw what I saw, Elizabeth. Out there tonight. We stared into the valley of death. I can no longer countenance, abandoning our parish, running away –

ELIZABETH. We are not running away!

CONSTANCE. You want to, what did you say, all return anew, aye. Too late by then. End of the summer? Not sure this lot will make it to the end of the weekend. Ignorance and hatred, they know not what they do. Perhaps what little light I have doesn't shine so bright these days, but I'm not prepared to take it away

ELIZABETH. Sister. You are allowed to doubt, and worry and question. But not here. Not now

PHILIPPA. There's no food. No power. And those lot out there –

CONSTANCE. We couldn't get them in when we offered tea and cake, but we've got to keep offering. And somebody needs to keep the place ticking over. Not as though this one can

ELIZABETH. You're not listening, Sister. There is nothing to be in charge of here, not any more. Even if you could sustain yourself, physically. You cannot, spiritually. We need to preserve our faith

CONSTANCE. I have nothing to preserve. Keep your weird science. That's not enough for me

THERESA. Sister Constance –

CONSTANCE. Don't Theresa. (*Beat.*) Look after them, won't you. I call you a silly girl but you're the, future of the convent

THERESA. I respect your choice

THERESA *hugs* CONSTANCE.

CONSTANCE *holds* PHILIPPA*'s hands*.

CONSTANCE. And you, Philippa – stay strong. You will follow in her footsteps –

ELIZABETH. No no no no no, this is nonsense, you're out of your mind. We're not going without you. We could never leave you behind

CONSTANCE. But you must

ELIZABETH. We go together, or not at all. We are all one flock

CONSTANCE. I will not hold you back. I've done enough of that. (*Beat*.) I blocked the vote after all

ELIZABETH. What?

CONSTANCE. I blocked the vote

PHILIPPA. No you didn't –

CONSTANCE. Yes I did –

PHILIPPA. Acting Mother don't listen to her –

CONSTANCE. Shut up. She doesn't speak for me. None of you do. I won't go to Ecuador. I voted you down before, cos I think you'll make, a terrible leader, Elizabeth, worst this place will ever have. Your only saving grace would be to take the others away right now. Right now. Ecuador means everything to them. And nothing to me. Nothing to me

CONSTANCE *exits*. *Pause*.

ELIZABETH. We leave her be. We, we, we need to figure out how to get away. Check the flights are still, no, it'll be fine, it has to be fine. The taxi. What about the taxi? That won't be coming, probably burning as we speak. Oh God, what do we do?

THERESA. I'll drive us

ELIZABETH. No Theresa –

THERESA. I will drive! The Old Mother's car, that hasn't been touched

ELIZABETH. You haven't got a licence

THERESA. But I can get us out of here. Sister Philippa, go to Sister Patricia. Make sure she's got a spare toothbrush

PHILIPPA. We'll be ready

PHILIPPA *exits*.

ELIZABETH. And what do I do?

THERESA. Pack your essentials too. And pray. Not for us. For Sister Constance. I hope you see one day what she's done for us. Go. Go! I'll bring the car around. Before they all come back!

ELIZABETH *exits.* THERESA *crouches by her lifeless friend.*

(*To* MARY.) I knew I had to say goodbye. I will pray for Sister Constance, Mary. But I'll also pray for you

THERESA *kisses her. She exits into the rain.*

The world sleeps until:

5 April – *Easter Sunday*

Almost dawn.

CONSTANCE *stares into space. She has her rosary beads loose in her hands. The projector and laptop from the opening scene lie awkwardly by her feet.*

MARY *wakes. She sits up. She looks around.*

CONSTANCE. You're alive then. (*Beat.*) Took Christ three days to come back from the dead, took you barely three hours

MARY. Where are the others?

CONSTANCE. Gone. They've gone

MARY. But you're, still here

CONSTANCE. You're a sharp one. (*Beat.*) What happened, you blow another fuse

MARY. No. I was, overwhelmed

CONSTANCE. By the Power of God? Sounds exhausting. I've been awake all night. Was gonna look at the slideshow again but. Power's still off. (*Beat.*) You just gonna sit there? Does the Lord not require some more heavenly chores? I had hoped, to be alone, a little longer. (*Beat.*) I suppose I am alone. You are, after all, 'no one', huh, s'just me, staring at a screen, all I get is my own reflection. Look at you, with your shoes off, why'd you do that, you want to feel what it's like? Mimicking the others, barefoot, wandering the forest. Hiding your mates

MARY. You don't believe it

CONSTANCE. No. No I don't. I don't know what occurred last night. Some kind of, mass hysteria. Maybe you were swept up in it too

MARY. I am a conduit. I am a vessel

CONSTANCE. You are a void. And so am I. I don't believe in miracles. Not any more

MARY. Is that why you stayed?

CONSTANCE. Nope. I stuck around because I blocked the vote

MARY. Is that what you told them?

CONSTANCE. Aye, that pushed them away

MARY. But you didn't block the vote

CONSTANCE. No

MARY. I blocked the vote

CONSTANCE (*beat*). What?

MARY. I blocked the vote. I know this now

CONSTANCE. No. It was Philippa, she, had a funny moment

MARY. I had a funny moment too

CONSTANCE (*beat*). You told us Patricia voted yes

MARY. She did. But I didn't submit her vote. I, submitted my own

CONSTANCE. Why?

MARY. God told me to

CONSTANCE. God, told you to blackball the. (*Chuckles*.) Well he's kept you busy

MARY. He has

CONSTANCE. Hiding the Reapers, smashing the relics, and what was His reasoning for this, did He not have faith in Elizabeth?

MARY. I think He has faith in all of you

CONSTANCE *chuckles again*.

It must be, His design. For it to lead to this

CONSTANCE. Lead to this? You and me? You and me in an empty (*Chuckles again*.)

MARY. What's so funny?

CONSTANCE. I've no idea. I thought I was doing some great and noble thing. Forcing the others away. Taking the fall for Philippa. Turns out, I'm taking the fall for you! For you. (*She can't stop laughing*.)

MARY. Sister?

CONSTANCE*'s laughter becomes crying*.

I will leave you, sister

CONSTANCE *is still crying*.

I will leave

MARY *goes to exit*.

The CHILD *appears at the door. They are not barefoot; they wear military boots which are traipsing muddy footprints*.

MARY *pauses, unable to work out if they are real or not. But this one is real alright*.

CONSTANCE *turns and sees the visitor*.

CONSTANCE. Oh! Welcome, um. Sorry I, always get emotional at Easter. Christ is dead and all that. I won't give any spoilers, but there's a big twist coming. What's your name? Are you lost? Can I fetch you some tea? We've got a camping stove set up in the kitchen. They can take away our power but they can't take away our tea. Mary, fetch the tea

The CHILD *produces a knife*.

CHILD. It's fetching me nothing

CONSTANCE (*beat*). No tea for you then

CHILD (*gestures to* MARY). Is this an instrument of our destruction?

CONSTANCE. Pardon?

CHILD. Is this an instrument of our destruction? We are wise to the tools of capitalism, they reek of the blood they spill

CONSTANCE. You're a Luddite

CHILD. We are the revolution. We are the momentum. Terms like 'Luddite' belittle our cause. We are the future. We are the progress

CONSTANCE. You're certainly a lot of things. I'll tell you what I am. Old enough to be your grandmother

CHILD. And I'm old enough to care. 'Bout my country. My lands, my birth right

CONSTANCE. There's no need to wave a knife around. You've missed the party. Your friends passed by last night

CHILD. Aye. I was there. But where are the cog-jobs?

CONSTANCE. The what?

CHILD. We came to gut them in the fields, pour the oil back into the soil they stole it from. You've hidden them. The robots

MARY. They're gone

CHILD (*jabbing at* MARY). Just this one left then

CONSTANCE. Hang on hang on. How do you know she's. Why d'you think she's a robot?

CHILD. Saw the photos online. One thing they're in the hospitals, the shops, but now they're in the churches?

CONSTANCE. And when's the last time you were in a church, eh? Just calm down. Tell me your name

CHILD. I am not one, I am many

CONSTANCE. Uh huh, well I'm Sister Constance, this is Mary

CHILD. Not talking to a cog-job

CONSTANCE. Look. If you leave right now, I won't be telling your parents, or anything like that

CHILD. They're in this fight as well! This is the beginning. The day of reckoning. We announced it on the streams, the last dusk, the new dawn, today's the day we take our future back. We reclaim the docks, the airports, we're gonna stop these things coming to our shores

CONSTANCE. The, airports?

CHILD. Do you know how much they're spending on these cog-jobs?

CONSTANCE. What's happening at the airports?

CHILD. Do you know how many they've assembled? Industry's dying, economy's tanking, but the elite build an army?

CONSTANCE. So you and friends build your own? You can't use violence to solve this. Nobody's gonna get hurt, are they? At the airports

CHILD. An eye for an eye. A tooth for a tooth

CONSTANCE. Now don't you go quoting scripture at me!

CHILD. We are the revolution. We are the momentum! You can't understand. You're safe in here, you're fed, get a bed. We don't even get that, but these things do?

CONSTANCE. I understand your pain, I do, it's tough, when things change

CHILD. So we're changing them back

CONSTANCE. But they're not the problem. They're just the wrong solution

CHILD. So you admit that it's wrong, it's unnatural, we are wise
    to the tools of capitalism, they reek of the blood they spill

CONSTANCE. Yes yes yes, you've said that already –

CHILD. I'll say it over and over again. I'll say it over and over
    again (*To* MARY.) Get on your knees

MARY. Please

CONSTANCE. Hey now –

CHILD. Shut up or you're next. (*To* MARY.) Get on your
    knees, or do I have to fix you already? (*Gestures with knife*.)

MARY. You're scaring me

CHILD. I'm scaring you? I'm scaring you?

    The CHILD *strikes* MARY. *She falls to the ground.*

    You're terrifying

    MARY *tries to get up and the* CHILD *strikes her again.*

MARY. I'm sorry. (*Beat*.) Forgive me

    The CHILD *strikes* MARY *again.*

CONSTANCE. Stop it. This isn't

CHILD. S'just a tool

CONSTANCE. She's not

CHILD. The wrong solution, that's what you said

CONSTANCE. I know I know, I'm, oh God

CHILD. We've got to gut the robot

CONSTANCE. But I'm the robot

CHILD (*pause*). What?

CONSTANCE. I'm the robot

CHILD (*beat*). No she's the robot

CONSTANCE. That's what we want you to think. Are all
    Luddites this stupid? She's just a decoy

MARY. Sister Constance –

CONSTANCE. Quiet! Far too pretty to be a robot, look at her. Now a nun robot, you're going to disguise it as an old crab like me, aren't you? It'll fit right in. Look at her feet. Count her toes. She doesn't have six. All robots have six toes, even you must know that. Or are you too thick to know

CHILD. Watch it

CONSTANCE. Come closer. Close as you dare –

MARY. Sister Constance –

CONSTANCE. I told you quiet, girl. Say another word and I'll beat you myself

CHILD. You telling me the truth?

CONSTANCE. I can only tell the truth. Look at how pathetic she is. The pain she feels. She's scared, she's lost, she's human. I feel nothing. Hit me. Hit me

The CHILD *hits* CONSTANCE *hard across the face.*

(*Beat.*) Nothing. You know what my eyes see? These x-ray eyes, I see your heart, quivering away. Too scared to do anything silly. So put that knife away

CHILD. No

CONSTANCE. Put it away

CHILD. I won't

CONSTANCE. Make absolutely sure. Cos I will call for back-up. I've hidden my robot sisters in the hills and they will come for me, they will come

CHILD. No

CONSTANCE *holds up her rosary to the heavens.*

CONSTANCE. My rosary! My circuitry! It's calling for them now! They're marching through the fields child, the future's marching in!

CHILD. Stop, stop, stop!

The CHILD *stabs* CONSTANCE *in the gut. Pause.*

The CHILD *steps back. Blood on the knife, blood on their hands.*

There's. Is this. Real?

CONSTANCE. Can't you tell?

CHILD. No I. (*Beat.*) You said

CONSTANCE. Aye. (*Beat.*) So you can forgive me too

The CHILD *runs out.*

CONSTANCE *collapses.* MARY *struggles up.*

MARY. Sister Constance

CONSTANCE. Nope, don't

MARY. We need to stop the bleeding

MARY *grabs the colourful scarf, she pushes it into the wound.*

CONSTANCE (*chuckles*). This was His plan. This was His plan

MARY. 'Let God's chosen fall.' You are His chosen. But I can't let you fall. We need to get you to a hospital

CONSTANCE. No time. You heard the child. The airports

MARY. I'll find them. I will assist you

CONSTANCE. No, no. It's really not as bad as it. Get this dirty cloth off me. Go

MARY. Sister Constance

CONSTANCE. If you don't save the others, then all of this, s'for nothing. And it's not for nothing. Find our sisters. You can save them. I trust you

MARY *leaves with the bloodied scarf – a relic for a new age.*

CONSTANCE *leans back and lets out a harrowing cry.*

Then, stillness. Almost at peace as she stares up. The world darkens.

Was this it then? This what you wanted? Funny way to go about it. But who am I to judge. (*Beat*.) Let me ask you, one thing, if I may. If you showed, the Old Mother, anything in Ecuador, anything at all, show me too. Please. Show me hope. Show me, strength. Show me tolerance. (*Pause*.) Or don't show me anything at all. Who am I to ask? I know who I am. I am, no one. 1, 1, 0, 1…

The projector flickers on.

It shines the light on the audience.

*

The stage is aglow.

CONSTANCE *stares in wonder as she's struck with divine revelation.*

We hear unearthly hymns as the Sisters of Grace form on the edge of the light.

We see every nun that CONSTANCE *ever knew.*

They all sing Hosanna, they witness the majesty.

The bell rings. As the CHILD *returns, the Holy Ghost is among us.*

We look to the heavens and:

CONSTANCE. Oh!

Lights out.

Praise Be To God.

A Nick Hern Book

Electric Rosary first published in Great Britain as a paperback original in 2022 by Nick Hern Books Limited, The Glasshouse, 49a Goldhawk Road, London W12 8QP

Cover image: Design & art direction by Studio Doug

Designed and typeset by Nick Hern Books, London
Printed in Great Britain by Mimeo Ltd, Huntingdon, Cambridgeshire PE29 6XX

A CIP catalogue record for this book is available from the British Library

ISBN 978 1 84842 937 6

www.nickhernbooks.co.uk

facebook.com/nickhernbooks

twitter.com/nickhernbooks